CENTRAL AMERICAN ECONOMIC INTEGRATION

Central American Economic Integration
THE POLITICS OF UNEQUAL BENEFITS

STUART I. FAGAN

Institute of International Studies
University of California, Berkeley

Standard Book Number 87725-115-0
Library of Congress Card Number 74-633252
© 1970 by the Regents of the University of California

FOREWORD

In international politics, as in other fields, the occur-
nce of an unprecedented event causes apprehension among some
d the desire to emulate the event among others. These charac-
ristics are typical of governments and men of action. Among
holars, however, the unexpected and the unprecedented give rise
two different reactions. Some wish to dispute that the event
s much significance, and they proceed to subsume it under con-
ptual and theoretical categories in vogue before the event took
ace. Others seek to use the innovation in world politics as
e core of a theory--and to seek the widest possible application
that theory.

The growth of the European common market, in the context
the movement toward regional unification in general, was such
event. It caused apprehension in Britain, Sweden, and Russia.
Latin America and Africa, by contrast, the potential power of
e European Economic Community triggered a desire for emulation--
th to reap the alleged benefits vouchsafed by larger markets
d to seek protection against the EEC's capacity to export and
port goods. Hence the early 1960's saw the creation of a num-
r of common markets and free trade areas in the regions marked
economic underdevelopment, reliance on primary goods produc-
on, and dependence on the fickle world economy. Among scholars
ere were those who shrugged their shoulders and, with the proper
ademic phrases and rhetorical questions, inquired "Quoi de
uf?" But there were also those who sought to develop theories
regional integration with applicability alike in West and East,
rth and South.

This book is concerned with the emulation of the common
rket idea in Central America. It is also concerned with test-
g some notions in the theory of integration, initially developed
the context of Western Europe, with respect to their applic-
ility in a different milieu.

Hence this study is of particular significance because
e common market idea was transplanted into apparently alien
il in the early 1960's, there to trigger many of the same prob-
ems and issues isolated and described in the Central American
xperience. The Latin American Free Trade Association, for ex-
mple, far from giving its members collective strength vis-à-vis
ird countries or other blocs, tended to languish. One of the
asons for its relative failure was the conviction of the smaller
and weaker members that the advantages of the freer trade accrued

disproportionately to the largest and most developed member nations. The West Indian Federation broke up in 1962 over a very similar crisis, and its successor--the Caribbean Free Trade Association--has yet to demonstrate its ability to give proportionate satisfaction to all its members. The East African common market all but collapsed because Tanganyika and Uganda feared to be left behind--under conditions of unregulated investment and free trade--by more dynamic Kenya. It was shored up only as a result of Kenyan willingness to make "side payments" to the other two partners in the form of special incentives to development. Efforts to create common markets in West Africa fell afoul of the unequal strength and economic endowment of the prospective members, and the common market setup in Central Africa seems perpetually on the brink of dissolution.

Why should this be so? The role of theory in the discussion of international integration and common markets is to describe, in uniform terms, _what_ has happened, to explain _why_ it had to happen, and to predict _how_ the trend or movement will fare in the future. The two major theoretical approaches--or pre-theories--developed in recent decades seek to make such statements, and they do so on the basis of experiences and insights gained from the study, initially, of regional integration in Western Europe. Transactionalists and neo-functionalists alike entertained low opinions of the capability of common markets in late developing regions to survive and contribute to political integration.[1] Experiences in the cases mentioned above seemed to provide grist for their mills. If the theories were any good at all, they seemed to predict success in developed countries and invariable failure of integration efforts among the poor nations.

The reasons for these predictions were quite clear. The low resource base of late developing countries seemed to impose

---

[1] For articles which summarize, formalize, and criticize the major pre-theoretical approaches to the study of regional integration, see the pieces by Hayward Alker, Donald Puchala, Joseph S. Nye, and Ernst B. Haas in _International Organization_, Vol. XXIV, No. 4 (Autumn 1970). The first neo-functional attempt at a general descriptive and predictive theory of regional integration via common markets is Ernst B. Haas and Philippe C. Schmitter, "Economics and Differential Patterns of Political Integration," _ibid._, Vol. XVIII, No. 4 (August 1964). Efforts at operationalizing the variables there proposed are contained in Mario Barrera and Ernst B. Haas, "The Operationalization of Some Variables Related to Regional Integration," _ibid._, Vol. XXIII, No. 1 (Winter 1969), and Philippe C. Schmitter, "Further Notes on Operationalizing Some Variables Related to Regional Integration," _ibid._, Vol. XXIII, No. 2 (Spring 1969).

sharp limits on the capability to defer benefits from common markets, to postpone the gratification of expectations. Therefore it was difficult to arrange for temporary special benefits for the most underdeveloped members of such groupings. Side payments could only be made with ease when the resource base was high, it was suggested. Moreover, the administrative structures of late developing countries were considered too poorly articulated to permit the making of decisions which would promote integration. Discussions of plans and projects could not be expected to lead to real planning. Hence free market forces would dominate in fact, thus further exacerbating the problems triggered by a low resource base and an unequal distribution of initial capabilities to profit from freer trade. Balance-of-payments problems would arise; rival fiscal measures would distort the meaning of regional free trade; compensatory joint decisions would not be made with respect to needed investments; agriculture would prove too difficult a sector to be included in a regional scheme; and the multinational corporation rather than local entrepreneurs would reap most of the benefits. Just because economic decisions were being made by a small group of officials with uncertain and changing ties to the political leadership, without enjoying the status of an established administrative apparatus, these problems would tend to swamp the fledgling integration scheme. Finally, it was feared that in the event of a distribution of benefits from freer trade which was perceived as inequitable by some of the participants, the mixture of low resources and poor administrative structure would combine to cause repeated "unequal distribution crises" which would probably lead to the collapse of the regional scheme. If the common market were based on an underlying political doctrine or a common regional ideology, this would not necessarily occur. But, unlike the Western European case, such ideologies do not tend to flourish in Latin America and Africa. Hence a common market once in the grips of an unequal distribution crisis would have no symbolic and ideological resources left to save itself.

Some writers sensed early in the game that such predictions were perhaps erroneous because they extrapolated conditions found useful in developed countries with respect to regional integration.[2] Others suggested that the fault lay with the effort to build an overly universal theory instead of providing for separate theories applicable to late developing countries.[3]

---

[2] For serious theoretical pieces casting doubt on the adequacy of these neo-functional predictions, see Joseph S. Nye, "Comparative Regional Integration: Concept and Measurement," International Organization, Vol. XXII, No. 4 (Autumn 1968), and Philippe C. Schmitter, "Three Neo-Functional Hypotheses about International Integration," ibid., Vol. XXIII, No. 1 (Winter 1969).

[3] Roger D. Hansen, "Regional Integration: Reflection on a Decade

In this continuing debate, the case of Central America is uniquely instructive. The Central American Common Market was in fact beset with all the difficulties described above. Yet it did not collapse. It is, of course, always possible that special and unique conditions intervened in this case which had not been recognized in any attempt at general theorizing. But we will not know this until we examine the actual facts and put them into the context of various explanatory and predictive constructs. Once we do this, it may be possible to explain the relative success of regional integration in Central America on the basis of the original pre-theories, to amend these theories, or to reject them in favor of a theory devised especially to deal with integration in Third World regions.

One of the most important steps in such an enterprise is to reconstruct the actual events which make up the frustrations and crises later manipulated analytically by theorists of integration. Mr. Fagan's treatment does just that. He enables us to see what the actors expected of one another, how they disappointed one another, what measures were proposed and occasionally accepted for satisfying the most disappointed without jettisoning the common market. He demonstrates that even in very underdeveloped countries it is possible for decision-makers to "learn," to satisfy their opposite numbers in a game of mutual recrimination and threat, stopping short of the actual destruction of the common enterprise. In short, this study provides the material for seriously evaluating the possibilities of adaptation, reformulation of attitudes and expectations, and redefining regional tasks in response to continuing crisis. It goes a long way toward showing how the neo-functional approach can be perfected and why it may not be necessary to devise separate theories for underdeveloped countries seeking to build common markets.

As such, Mr. Fagan's study is a companion piece to a number of related studies. All were undertaken in the context of the project entitled Studies in International Integration, housed in the Institute of International Studies of the University of California, Berkeley. Some of these studies, still to be completed, deal with cognate phenomena in Central and West Africa. Others deal with Latin America, and several are designed to revise and expand the neo-functional approach to the study of regional integration so as to take direct cognizance of the trends and events described by Mr. Fagan.[4] The theoretical and the

---

of Theoretical Efforts," World Politics, Vol. XXI, No. 2 (January 1969).

[4]These formulations are contained in Philippe C. Schmitter, "A Revised Theory of International Integration," International

empirical work connected with this project was, from beginning to end, a group enterprise. It was informed by the commitment of the participants not to permit theory to push aside the facts the field work seemed to uncover, but it was inspired by the hope that not all field work need be destructive of all abstract theorizing. The participants in this project have included, in addition to Mr. Fagan, Professors Philippe C. Schmitter and Abdul A. Jalloh, Dr. Aaron Segal, Dr. Branislav Gosovic, Mukund Untawale, and Daniel Baedeker. It was at all times my greatest pleasure to participate in their collective and individual endeavors.

On behalf of this group I wish to express my gratitude to Dr. Miguel Wionczek, Dr. Carlos Castillo, and Mr. Abraham Bennaton for having given us the benefit of their advice on matters relating to Central American integration. All mistakes remain ours.

Ernst B. Haas

Berkeley, California
September 1970

Organization, Vol. XXIV, No. 4 (Autumn 1970), and "La dinámica de contradicciones y la conducción de crisis en la integración centroamericana," Revista de la Integración, No. 5, November 1969.

ACKNOWLEDGMENTS

I wish to express particular thanks to Dr. Ernst Haas, Director of the Studies of International Integration Project, for his stimulation, guidance, and encouragement throughout the preparation of this monograph.

I also want to thank Mr. Paul Gilchrist, Editor for the Institute of International Studies, for the patience with which he corrected my many errors.

Finally, I am grateful to Mrs. Kathy Wilson, Miss Bojana Ristich, and Miss Heide Beuter, who typed the various drafts of the monograph.

Stuart I. Fagan

CONTENTS

LIST OF TABLES

INTRODUCTION

The first efforts to achieve some economic cooperation among the five Central American countries were initiated by a closely knit group of economists associated with the Economic Commission for Latin America (ECLA). During the early 1950's, ECLA was instrumental in creating several regional institutions in Central America, training politically neutral local técnicos, negotiating a series of bilateral treaties in the area, and sponsoring research on the economic potentialities of the region. Acting on this foundation and spurred by ECLA, representatives of the five Central American countries in 1958 signed the Multilateral Treaty on Free Trade and Central American Integration, which provided for the development of a free trade zone within ten years by means of periodic multilateral negotiations. At the same time, they signed the Agreement on Central American Integration Industries, which was intended to help achieve a more or less equitable distribution of the benefits derived from free trade. One year later, the five states signed the Central American Agreement on Tariff Equalization, designed to establish a common external tariff within five years--also through periodic, item-by-item negotiations. These agreements were followed in 1960 by the more extensive General Treaty of Central American Economic Integration.

In July 1969 war broke out between El Salvador and Honduras. It was the only war in recent history waged by one common market member against one of its partners. The conflict brought to a halt at least temporarily what appeared to have been ten years of cooperation among the five Central American countries.

In fact, however, the war did not interrupt an integration process which had been characterized by significant spillovers in tasks, by a growth in the mutual responsiveness of national elites, or by the delegation of increasing authority to regional institutions. Even before the July war, the Central American Common Market (CACM) was on the verge of collapse, primarily because of its inability to deal satisfactorily with the problem of unbalanced development. The war reinforced prevailing political and economic trends in Central America rather than interrupting them.

- - - - - - - - - -

The overall objective of this paper is threefold: first, to present a detailed, comprehensive description of the process

1

of Central American integration; second, by applying concepts developed by integration theorists, to abstract trends from this integration process which are grounded in the facts; and third, by analysis of past trends, to make some projections about prospects for integration in Central America in the near and not so near future.

I. BALANCED DEVELOPMENT, FUNCTIONALISM, AND THE CACM

Achievements of the General Treaty: 1961-1965

In signing the General Treaty of Economic Integration in late 1960, the Central American countries committed themselves to establish immediate free trade with one another for nearly all regionally produced items. In addition, they agreed to reach a settlement within five years on the relatively few articles exempted from immediate free trade. They already had agreed to common external rates for a substantial number of items in the Agreement on the Equalization of Import Duties signed in 1959, and had committed themselves to the progressive equalization of duties on products temporarily exempted. Together, these two treaties provided for immediate free movement for most Central American products within a customs union which was gradually to be established.

The General Treaty also included several less firm commitments. The signatories "endorsed" the provisions of the previously signed Regime for Integration Industries, and promised to sign additional protocols specifying the plants initially to be covered by the agreement.[1] They agreed to establish a Central American Bank for Economic Integration (CABEI) to finance and promote "regionally balanced, integrated economic growth."[2] And they pledged themselves to sign a protocol "to ensure as soon as possible a reasonable equalization" of their laws regulating tax incentives for industrial development.[3] However, in depositing the General Treaty, the five countries definitively committed themselves only to free trade and to a common external tariff for a large number of items; each of the other pledges required the negotiation, ratification, and deposit of separate protocols to be effected.

By and large, by the mid-1960's, the member countries fulfilled the legal obligations entered into as a consequence of

---

[1] General Treaty for Central American Economic Integration (Guatemala: Permanent Secretariat of Central American Economic Integration, 1964), Article XVII.

[2] Ibid., Article XVIII.

[3] Ibid., Article XIX.

the two treaties. By 1965, there was free trade for 94 percent of the items in the Central American tariff schedule (NAUCA), encompassing 95 percent of the value of intra-regional trade. Although the five members were (and continued to be) unable to agree on free trade for the few remaining items (consisting largely of sugar and refined petroleum products), trade of these slowly declined as each country began to attain self-sufficiency in their production.[4]

The five countries enjoyed almost as much success in establishing common external rates. By the mid-1960's there were common rates for 98 percent of the items in NAUCA. The new rates were intended to stimulate industrial development by means of import substitution without entirely disregarding their traditional revenue producing and balance-of-payments functions. Therefore, they were high for consumer goods that were manufactured in the region or that might be produced there in the near future, moderate for consumer goods not produced in the area, and low for raw materials, intermediate goods, and capital goods unavailable in the region. Overall, the new tariff was higher than the average of the previous rates.[5]

The members were not entirely successful in reaching agreement on a common external tariff, however. The 2 percent of the items which remained nonequalized, consisting largely of automotive vehicles, petroleum and petroleum products, wheat and wheat flour, and a variety of electrical appliances, represented 19.4 percent of the value of the region's total imports in 1965.[6] The member countries could not agree on common rates for these

---

[4] For a more detailed analysis of the operation of the system of internal free trade for Central American products, see Andrew B. Wardlaw, "The Operations of the Central American Common Market" (Guatemala City: Regional Office for Central America and Panama, Agency for International Development, U.S. Department of State, 1966), mimeo.

[5] Roger Hansen, in Central America: Regional Integration and Economic Development (Washington: National Planning Association, Studies in Development Progress, No. 1, 1967), pp. 26-28 and 51, discusses the structure of the new tariff in detail. See also Carlos Castillo, Growth and Integration in Central America (New York: Praeger, 1966), pp. 84-85.

[6] SIECA (Permanent Secretariat of Central American Economic Integration), Carta Informativa, No. 66 (April 1967), Anexo Estadístico No. 61. By 1967, the figure had dropped to 15 percent (SIECA, Carta Informativa, No. 92 [June 1969], Anexo Estadístico No. 87).

items in part because of their fiscal importance: they accounted
for approximately 27 percent of the total tariff revenues, on the
average, collected by four of the five members.[7] But there were
additional reasons why tariff equalization of these items was
difficult. E.g., each of the five countries wanted its own re-
finery, and derived substantial revenue from taxes on the sale
of petroleum products; only Guatemala grew wheat, and it pressed
for greater protection than the others were willing to grant.
Finally, the main obstacle to agreement on common rates for several of the remaining articles was the absence of any regional
regulation of assemblage activities (pledged in the Common Fiscal
Incentives Agreement).[8]

In response to the larger market and new tariff, the
volume of intra-Central American trade rose steadily from $33
million in 1960 to $174 million in 1966. Regional trade as a
percentage of total exports expanded from 7.4 percent to more
than 20 percent.[9]

The regional policy of import substitution appeared to
enjoy some success. The composition of regional trade changed,
manufactures and chemical products replacing foodstuffs as the
primary items regionally traded.[10] Imports from third countries
rose from 18 percent of the regional gross domestic product in
1961 to 21 percent in 1966. But in the context of an overall
increased demand, imports of consumer goods, especially light
manufactures, fell. Accompanying the process of industrial
growth, imports of capital goods and advanced intermediate goods
increased.[11]

---

[7]SIECA, Comentarios sobre los rubros pendientes de equiparación
arancelaria (Nota de la Secretaría), SIECA/CE-XV/64, Guatemala,
June 1965, p. 2.

[8]Wardlaw, pp. 50-54; INTAL (Instituto para la Integración de
América Latina), La integración económica de América Latina
(Buenos Aires: 1968), pp. 318-321.

[9]IIEJI (Instituto Interamericano de Estudios Jurídicos Inter-
nacionales), Derecho comunitario centroamericano (San José,
Costa Rica: 1968), p. 68. By 1968 intra-Central American trade
reached $260 million, an increase of approximately 650 percent
over 1961. See SIECA, Carta Informativa, No. 93 (July 1969), for
the most recent zonal trade figures.

[10]Wardlaw, pp. 18-25.

[11]Vincent Cable, "Problems in the Central American Common Market," Review, Bank of London and South America, Vol. 3, No. 30
(June 1969), pp. 337-338.

Since most of the new industries established were assembly plants in which little value was added to the final products by Central American materials inputs or production processes, increases in regional industrial production probably resulted in little saving of foreign exchange--at least during the early 1960's.[12] In addition, the growth of assembly industries, stimulated by the liberal application of national industrial incentives laws in some of the countries, undermined government revenues, which were heavily dependent on import duties.[13] Fortunately, favorable international markets for most of the region's traditional exports during this period lessened the fiscal costs and balance-of-payments pressures which had been expected as a consequence of integration.

In contrast to these substantial accomplishments, the member countries failed to fulfill their pledge with regard to the integration industries scheme. As initially conceived along with the Multilateral Treaty of 1958, the scheme had several objectives. First, it was intended to promote industrialization by attracting to the region large, basic industries which required immediate access to a large market to operate economically. Firms designated as integration plants were to receive substantial benefits, including immediate regional free trade, tariff protection, and exemption from duties on the import of raw materials and semi-manufactured inputs for ten years. A second objective was to ensure balance among countries; thus the provision that integration industries were to be distributed on the "bases of reciprocity and equity." According to Carlos Castillo, present Secretary-General of the CACM, "the question of the possible unfavorable effects of free trade on balance among countries was to be solved by limiting the free trade privilege in the case of major industries, so as to apportion them equitably among the member countries."[14] Officials of the Economic Commission for Latin America (ECLA) recognized even in the late 1950's that the issue of balanced industrial development would create grave problems if it were not dealt with at an early stage in the integration process. They designed the integration industries scheme in part to

---

[12] Several examples of these "industrias de fantasmas" are given in Meldon E. Levine, "The Private Sector and the Common Market," Woodrow Wilson School of Public and International Affairs, Princeton University, October 1965 (unpublished), pp. 42-43.

[13] Import duties both as a percentage of import value and of government revenue declined between 1961-1965 in large part as a result of national competition in the granting of tariff and tax exemptions to new industries and the overall policy of import substitution (Hansen, Central America, pp. 82-83).

[14] Castillo, p. 144.

prevent greater industrial disparity within the region. Finally, the integration industries scheme was intended to extend free trade beyond the few items covered by the Multilateral Treaty.

The scheme did not succeed in fulfilling these objectives. With the signing of the General Treaty and the achievement of generalized free trade, it could no longer serve to extend free trade nor to achieve balance among countries, at least not by limiting free trade.[15] Nor did the scheme help to promote basic industrialization. As a result of several negative factors, there were few applications for integration status. (At present only two plants are in operation.) Generalized free trade and a common tariff reduced the attractiveness of the scheme to potential applicants. In addition, designation procedures were lengthy, consisting of application to the Permanent Secretariat of Central American Economic Integration (SIECA), technical studies by the Central American Institute for Industrial Research and Technology (ICAITI), the drafting of a protocol, passage by the Executive and Economic Councils, and national ratification and deposit by at least three member countries, with the final outcome uncertain. More important, from the very beginning it was difficult to attract capital for integration plants. The United States, claiming that the scheme would lead to the creation of monopolies, refused to allow its funds in the Central American Bank for Economic Integration (CABEI) to be loaned to integration industries. Until recently, the Inter-American Development Bank (IDB) followed a similar policy. Moreover, El Salvador, Guatemala, and Costa Rica, believing that they were benefitting from a free flow of investment funds, at first opposed any multi-national allocation of industries. With only two plants in operation, the scheme has not succeeded in promoting basic industrialization, or in creating a balance among countries in the apportionment of industries.

The same day that the five countries signed the General Treaty they established the Central American Bank for Economic Integration. CABEI enjoyed considerable financial success from its formation. Its resources multiplied as it attracted loans from the U.S., the Inter-American Development Bank, and several foreign countries.[16] It also became the administrator of the

---

[15] Ibid., pp. 144-145.

[16] It had attracted loans from Mexico, Spain, France, Italy, Holland, and Switzerland by the end of 1967 (INTAL, La integración economica. . ., p. 384). See Philippe Schmitter, "The Process of Central American Integration: Spill-Over or Spill-Around?" (Berkeley: University of California, Institute of International Studies), mimeographed, pp. 23-25, for a more extended discussion of the performance of CABEI.

Fund for Central American Integration, established in 1965 with $35 million from the U.S. and $7 million from the member governments. By the end of 1967 CABEI had allocated more than $110 million in loans, almost equally divided between the public and private sectors.

CABEI had less success in fulfilling one of its primary objectives--the promotion of balanced development. As Table 1 indicates, it allocated the largest shares of its funds to the two least developed members, Honduras and Nicaragua. However, close analysis of the figures for the years prior to 1967, for which more detailed data are available, reveals that the shares received by the two countries were considerably smaller when calculations are based on loans disbursed rather than on loans allocated.[17] Even on the basis of loans allocated, Honduras ranked fourth in loans granted for actual industrial and infrastructure investments. The bank allocated two-thirds of the funds available for feasibility studies to Honduras. But feasibility studies must be followed by additional requests for loans intended for subsequent investments. From the beginning the problem was not that CABEI was unwilling to give priority to Honduran projects, or that it was unable to do so as a consequence of opposition from other members. Rather, Honduras simply submitted few projects for consideration. An overall low technical capacity, administrative inertia and disorganization, a relatively small and (with the notable exception of the "Turcos" in the Northeast) undynamic industrial group, and external economies, which under free market conditions led to the concentration of new investment in the traditional regional centers, account for Honduras' inability to take full advantage of CABEI funds.

Finally, although in 1962 the member countries fulfilled their pledge to sign the Common Fiscal Incentives Agreement, that convention was not in effect by the mid-1960's. Honduras refused to deposit it without revisions. The designers of the CACM intended the convention on fiscal incentives to stimulate industrial development, while at the same time prevent the kind of competition for new industries which would undermine national balance-of-payments and government revenues. But the main provision of the agreement--regional equalization of incentives to industry--conflicted with its other principle of balanced development, which was held to be crucial--especially by Honduras.

Two provisions in the convention favored the less developed members. First, industries were to be classified by national criteria during the first seven years.[18] Since the less developed

_____

[17] Wardlaw, p. 86.

[18] Agreement on Fiscal Incentives for Industrial Development, Article 25. (U.S. Agency for International Development, Regional

Table 1

CENTRAL AMERICAN BANK FOR ECONOMIC INTEGRATION LOANS APPROVED BY COUNTRIES AND SECTORS THROUGH 31 DECEMBER 1967

(in thousands of U.S. dollars)

Destination of Loan	Central America		Guatemala		El Salvador		Honduras		Nicaragua		Costa Rica	
	No.	Value	No.	Value	No.	Value	No.	Value	No.	Value	No.	Value
TOTAL	180	110,503.2	40	21,361.2	34	18,193.8	43	22,721.0	37	28,256.8	26	19,970.4
Studies	35	4,690.0	3	153.2	4	162.0	17	3,068.7	9	1,104.4	2	201.8
Investment	145	105,813.2	37	21,208.0	30	18,031.8	26	19,652.3	28	27,152.4	24	19,768.6
Industrial[a]	130	47,111.0	32	8,478.2	26	10,831.8	26	8,224.4	26	13,399.2	20	6,177.4
Studies	16	1,081.0	3	153.2	2	12.0	5	878.2	5	25.8	1	11.8
Investment	114	46,030.0	29	8,325.0	24	10,819.8	21	7,346.2	21	13,373.4	19	6,165.6
Infrastructure	38	53,392.2	3	10,633.0	6	5,362.0	15	12,746.6	10	12,857.6	4	11,793.0
Studies	19	3,609.0	--	--	2	150.0	12	2,190.5	4	1,078.6[d]	1	190.0
Investment	19	49,783.2	3	10,633.0	4	5,212.0[b]	3	10,556.1[c]	6	11,779.0	3	11,603.0[e]
Housing	12	10,000.0	5	2,250.0	2	2,000.0	2	1,750.0	1	2,000.0	2	2,000.0
Investment	12	10,000.0	5	2,250.0	2	2,000.0	2	1,750.0	1	2,000.0	2	2,000.0

[a] Includes loans for hotels for $2,014.8 thousands.

[b] Includes $260.0 thousands for supply of cereals and $202.0 thousands for university education.

[c] Includes $49.1 thousands for air transport and $1,000.0 thousands for electric service.

[d] Includes $645.0 thousands for education and $481.0 thousands for electric service.

[e] Includes $1,103.0 thousands for electric service.

Source: INTAL, La integración económica . . ., p. 386.

members by definition would have fewer types of industry, they would be able to classify a greater number of them as "new" and could grant correspondingly greater concessions.[19] This advantage was to disappear in the eighth year, when the basis for industrial classification would switch to regional criteria.[20] Second, the agreement allowed Honduras and Nicaragua to grant "new" industries exemptions from taxes on income, profits, stock, and property for two and one extra years respectively.[21] Honduras came to believe that these provisions were inadequate to promote balanced development. [The controversy over the issue of common fiscal incentives is discussed in detail below.]

Institutional Structure of Integration

In addition to these commitments in several issue areas, the General Treaty set up several organs to serve as the institutional structure of the CACM: an Economic Council consisting of the Ministers of Economy; an Executive Council made up of one titular official and one alternate appointed by each government; and a permanent secretariat (SIECA) headed by a Secretary-General appointed by the Economic Council.[22] Although ambiguous as to the specific tasks assigned to each of these bodies, the treaty established the Economic Council as the supreme integration organ. It gave to the Economic Council the authority to examine the work of the Executive Council, to serve as a final recourse for members dissatisfied with Executive Council decisions, to adopt the budget, and to appoint the Secretary-General. Although the treaty charged the Economic Council with "integrating the Central American economies," it also authorized the Executive Council to propose additional treaties required to achieve economic integration, as well as to apply and administer the treaty provisions and to resolve problems arising from their application. It did not restrict SIECA to the task of servicing the two councils in a strictly technical sense, but authorized it to supervise implementation of the several integration treaties and any subsequent resolutions passed by the councils.

Office for Central America and Panama, Economic Integration Treaties of Central America [Guatemala City, 1966]).

[19] This explanation is given by Wardlaw, p. 89.

[20] Agreement on Fiscal Incentives, Article 24.

[21] Ibid., Fifth Temporary Article.

[22] General Treaty, Articles XX through XXIV deal with the organizational structure of the CACM.

According to the formally prescribed system of voting, the Economic Council was to determine unanimously, before ruling on an issue, whether the matter was to be decided by the concurring votes of all its members or by a simple majority. The Executive Council was empowered to pass resolutions by a majority vote, but in the event of disagreement, the matter was to be referred to the Economic Council for a final ruling. However, all major policy innovations would require the ratification and deposit of treaties or protocols.

In practice, SIECA became, as one observer of the CACM has noted, "the true engine of integration."[23] When conflicts over questions of national origin, labeling, tax discrimination, unfair trade practices, and the like--so-called "Common Market problems"--interrupted trade, SIECA was the key institution for settling them and reestablishing free trade. It arranged meetings of national economic officials of the parties in dispute. It handled the administrative tasks for these meetings and presented its own study of the issues and recommendations for their resolution. Occasionally, it even arranged agreements by telephone. When members could not resolve a "Common Market problem" on their own or through direct meetings or other means established by SIECA, SIECA or one of the parties concerned brought the issue to the Executive Council. On these occasions, SIECA presented the overall case to the council, the parties had their say, and the council generally met behind closed doors to try to reach some consensus, although at times it resolved "Common Market problems" by simple majority vote. Council decisions were based on SIECA recommendations. The council referred problems on which there was no easy agreement to a subcommittee consisting of secondary national economic officials, in which SIECA participated. The working group often requested that SIECA study the issue further. The studies carried out by SIECA evidenced technical competence, a regional point of view, and political shrewdness, and served as the basis for the conflict's later resolution.

SIECA performed additional tasks as well. It carried out studies and prepared protocols assigned to it by the councils as well as on its own. In addition to "Common Market problems," the Executive Council assigned SIECA to study proposed protocols on which there was no agreement. SIECA also collaborated with the councils in the writing of numerous resolutions and bylaws. Finally, it was the chief promoter and organizer of several regional meetings of various national officials.

---

[23]Dusan Sidjanski, Dimensiones institucionales de la integración latinoamericana (Buenos Aires: INTAL, 1967), p. 109. See his excellent description of the operations of CACM institutions, pp. 101-123. Also IIEJI, Derecho comunitario centroamericano, pp. 188-200.

The Executive Council, consisting of the Vice-Ministers of Economy of the five countries, spent the bulk of its time ruling on charges of violations of free trade on the basis of SIECA's recommendations. From the beginning, it operated with an informal style of decision-making uncharacteristic of traditional international organizations. Moreover, member countries almost never appealed its decisions on "Common Market problems" to the Economic Council, even though the Economic Council was constitutionally enabled to use the unanimity formula to permit a member government dissatisfied with the operation of the Common Market to escape censure by the majority. In practice the Executive Council made nearly all decisions having to do with complaints concerning the operation of the market. It also served as a transmission belt to the Economic Council. It prepared and negotiated resolutions and drafts of regional agreements preliminary to their consideration by the higher organ. These tasks, as indicated above, were carried out with the assistance of SIECA.

The Economic Council dealt with issues referred to it by SIECA or the Executive Council--issues incapable of being resolved at those lower decision-making levels--as well as the final negotiation of protocols. However, signature of a protocol by Economic Council members did not mean its rapid implementation. Passage by the Economic Council was only a recommendation to the member states to ratify and deposit the agreement.

By the mid-1960's the principle Common Market organs had expanded the number and types of their activities, even though significant pledges made in the General Treaty remained unfulfilled. The number of demands on the councils rose steadily, and they began to meet more and more often. In part, this was in response to the rise in problems brought on by increasing trade. But SIECA itself was partly responsible for the additional activity. It was continually on the lookout for problems which it brought to the attention of the two councils and concerning which it made recommendations. SIECA's budget and staff doubled, and the number of its departments grew. Its recommendations, if adopted, would have expanded the scope of integration considerably.

SIECA's most significant task expansion occurred in 1965 when the Economic Council requested that the Joint Planning Mission (JOPLAN) be incorporated into it. JOPLAN had been created in 1962 following an earlier council request to the Economic Commission for Latin America (ECLA), the Inter-American Development Bank (IDB), and the Organization of American States (OAS). It provided technical assistance to the newly formed national planning boards and classified national economic information.[24]

---

[24] Schmitter, "The Process of CA Integration," p. 34. Schmitter describes and analyzes the development of JOPLAN in detail.

However, despite the existence of JOPLAN and several meetings of the national planning directors, the CACM was still without any regional industrial planning or coordination by the mid-1960's.

Several other institutions became involved in the integration process. Some of these organizations predated the CACM, but were reinvigorated by it and changed and expanded their tasks in response to it. Nye has referred to this process in which "less active institutions are stimulated to greater activity by the success of more active institutions" as "demonstration effect spillover"; Schmitter has called the product of this process "integrative fallout."[25] ICAITI, increasingly requested by the Executive Council and other agencies to carry out technical studies on regional problems related to integration, the Central American Institute for Public Administration (ICAP, formerly ESAPAC), and the Nutrition Institute of Central America and Panama (INCAP) were institutions which experienced "fallout." Another was the Organization of Central American States (ODECA), which was founded by foreign ministers from the five countries in 1951 with the objective of rapid political unity, but with almost no authority to achieve it, and which was paralyzed by political conflict for the next decade.[26] Concerned about being left behind in the integration process, ODECA reorganized itself in 1962 and attempted to become involved in regional efforts in areas other than the strictly economic sector covered by the CACM. By 1965, it had created several new organs to deal with regional coordination in the fields of labor, social security, statistics, public health, and tourism, and had acquired considerable financial backing from USAID. These organs carried out technical studies and held several meetings, but national officials continued to retain all of their authority over decisions in these issue-areas.

The apparent success of the CACM not only served to reinvigorate older organizations, but also stimulated the founding of new institutions. CABEI is an example of a newly created institution with ties to the CACM. Its Board of Directors includes the Ministers of Economy of the five states as well as the presidents of the five Central Banks. On the other hand, several of the new organizations have no formal ties to the Common Market. The tie between the Monetary Council and the CACM, for example, is tenuous. The General Treaty instructs the Central Banks only to "cooperate closely" in order to prevent exchange rate specula-

---

[25] Joseph Nye, "Central American Economic Integration" in Joseph Nye, ed., International Regionalism (Boston: Little, Brown, 1968), p. 409; Schmitter, "The Process of CA Integration," pp. 56-64.

[26] For a history of the activities and difficulties of ODECA, see IIEJI, Derecho comunitario centroamericano, pp. 257-290.

tion which could adversely affect the Common Market.[27] Given the degree of autonomy from national political authorities enjoyed by each of the Central Banks, the Ministers of Economy, even had they so desired, could not have included them within the institutional structure they created in 1960. However, the Central Banks, acting on their own, had met several times during the 1950's to consider possible areas of cooperation.[28] They even considered a number of proposals to establish a mechanism for interregional clearings, but failed to reach agreement on any of them. Since the level of commercial activity during the 1950's among the five states was extremely low and since regional payments had long been cleared easily through New York banking houses, there was no pressing need for such a mechanism. However, following the implementation of the General Treaty and perhaps anticipating future problems, the presidents of the Central Banks, again acting independently, created the Central American Clearing House to encourage the use of national currencies in regional transactions. By 1965 the new mechanism cleared more than 80 percent of interregional trade and was operating smoothly despite exchange restrictions imposed earlier by Guatemala and El Salvador.

Encouraged by the success of the Clearing House, the presidents of the Central Banks, once more acting on their own, in 1964 signed an "Agreement for the Establishment of the Central American Monetary Union." As Gonzalez del Valle has noted, this was not a formal treaty but "an agreement setting up ways and means for voluntary cooperation among independent national institutions."[29] The agreement's major objectives were to promote the coordination of the monetary, exchange, and credit policies of the five countries and to progressively create the foundations for a monetary union. It set up a Monetary Council, consisting of the five Central Bank presidents, an Executive Secretariat, and several advisory committees. During its first few years of operation, however, the council carried out no new activities, with the exception of a study of payments problems in Central America.

---

[27] General Treaty, Article X.

[28] This account is based on the excellent analysis of recent efforts at Central American monetary integration in Jorge Gonzalez del Valle, "Monetary Integration in Central America: Achievements and Expectations," Journal of Common Market Studies, Vol. V, No. 1 (September 1966), pp. 13-25. See also John Parke Young, Central American Monetary Union (Guatemala: U.S. Department of State, AID, ROCAP, 1965).

[29] Gonzalez del Valle, p. 20.

The formation of the CACM and the growth in regional trade also inspired the formation of private regional organizations, the most important being the Central American Federation of Chambers of Industry, the Central American Federation of the Chambers of Commerce, and the Central American Textile Federation. Individuals, private firms, and organizations still tried to influence integration policy directly through their national economic officials rather than through private regional organizations or regional authorities, but the new institutions signified the private sector's acceptance of the CACM as a fact to be reckoned with. In general, from 1961 to 1965, the opinions of the national industrial associations (with the exception of the Honduran association) moved from neutral or indifferent to strongly favorable, and those of the chambers of commerce from opposed to neutral, or at least to acceptance of the CACM as an irreversible development.

Summary of the Integration Process Until 1965

By the mid-1960's there existed a large and growing number of regional institutions in Central America encompassing an increasing number of tasks. Taken together, the scope of their interests was very broad, ranging from free trade to nutrition. Most of these organizations were not subject to the authority of a central regional body, but existed more or less autonomously. In a sense, the integration effort was not one but several efforts, each issue-area being taken up by a different, largely autonomous institution. In only one issue-area did government representatives sitting on the boards of regional institutions engage in mutual decision-making.[30] The exception was the area of interregional trade. In accord with the members' original

---

[30] Schmitter has referred to this type of integration process as the "spill-around" syndrome. The spill-around syndrome is "characterized by a proliferation of independent efforts at regional coordination in distinct functional spheres--i.e., an expansion in the scope of regional tasks--without, however, a concomitant devolution of authority to a single collective body--i.e., without an increase in the level of decision-making. New issue areas become 'collectivized' or 'regionalized' and transaction rates increase impressively, but there is no transcendence, no fundamental redefinition of norms and goals, no emergence of a new and wider sense of community loyalty. The new institutions sprout up or are revitalized in a more or less uncoordinated manner. Each is relatively autonomous from the other, depending upon different sources of national, political and financial support, as well as external aid and encouragement in the Central American case" (Schmitter, "The Process of CA Integration," p. 66).

commitments, CACM organs from 1961-1965 prevented any of the five countries from interfering with free trade. SIECA even developed some de facto executive powers for dealing with obstructions to free trade. By 1965, it appeared that most national decision-makers and private groups viewed free trade as fundamentally an economic matter and an irreversible fact.

The Issue of Balanced Development: Economic Considerations

One of the most striking characteristics of the CACM during its initial years was the extent to which it relied on the free operation of market forces (once internal trade barriers wer down and a protected market created) to achieve economic development. Within a short time after the establishment of the Common Market, these unregulated market forces seemed to operate in a way which resulted in the distribution of unequal economic benefits to the member countries.

The volume of interregional trade rose very rapidly durin the market's early years. Unfortunately, the distribution and co position of that trade favored the more industrial members. As Table 2 indicates, Honduras and Nicaragua experienced steadily growing trade deficits with their more industrialized partners. Honduras ran a large deficit on manufactured goods, many of which were highly protected, and a surplus on agricultural products, which did not enjoy protection.[31] Nicaragua experienced trade de icits in all major categories except vegetable oils and raw materials. Its growing deficits in regional trade became expecially serious for Nicaragua once the favorable conditions that it enjoyed for its exports to third countries during 1961-64 began to deteriorate and its trade deficit with these countries began to rise sharply. Overall, both of the less developed members appeare to experience trade diversion rather than trade creation as a consequence of the CACM.

Perhaps more important and partly responsible for these imbalances, both less developed members were unsuccessful, relative to the more industrial countries, in attracting foreign industrial investment. As a consequence of historical location factors, the failure of the integration industries scheme, the free-for-all national competition in granting concessions to foreign investors, and the limited success of CABEI in helping the less developed members, most large new firms established themselve in Guatemala City, San Salvador, or San José. Even some smaller plants, which might have been set up in Honduras and Nicaragua on the basis of their national markets alone, were attracted by

---

[31]Cable, p. 340. Cable examines the economic benefits and losses for each of the five countries due to their membership in the CACM. This section draws on his excellent analysis.

Table 2

TRADE BALANCES: INTRA-CENTRAL AMERICAN TRADE, 1961-1968

(in millions of U.S. dollars)

	Guatemala	El Salvador	Honduras	Nicaragua	Costa Rica
1961					
Imports	8.9	14.7	6.4	2.9	4.0
Exports	8.6	15.0	8.6	1.8	2.2
Balance	-0.3	0.3	2.2	-1.1	-1.8
1962					
Imports	11.2	22.0	8.9	5.3	3.3
Exports	8.7	18.7	12.1	3.5	1.7
Balance	-2.5	-3.3	3.2	-1.8	-1.6
1963					
Imports	19.7	27.9	13.2	7.3	3.8
Exports	17.3	30.2	12.5	4.8	3.9
Balance	-2.4	2.3	-0.7	-2.5	0.1
1964					
Imports	26.4	39.2	18.0	14.3	8.3
Exports	29.6	36.8	16.4	7.1	15.4
Balance	3.2	-2.4	-1.6	-7.2	7.1
1965					
Imports	31.5	42.4	25.5	21.4	14.7
Exports	35.6	45.4	20.5	12.4	18.2
Balance	4.1	3.0	-5.0	-9.0	3.5
1966					
Imports	33.8	52.0	34.0	31.6	23.2
Exports	50.8	58.6	19.5	16.2	25.2
Balance	17.0	6.6	-14.5	-15.4	2.0
1967					
Imports	42.1	54.5	40.8	42.4	34.2
Exports	57.9	79.2	23.4	18.2	26.9
Balance	15.8	24.7	-17.4	-24.2	-7.3
1968					
Imports	49.4	65.7	48.4	46.2	49.5
Exports	67.0	85.7	30.3	24.6	36.2
Balance	17.6	20.0	-18.1	-21.6	-13.3

Source: SIECA, Carta Informativa, No. 93, pp. 18-20.

external economies and established instead in the more industrial countries. Initially, neither Honduras nor Nicaragua appeared to gain economic benefits from free trade, especially relative to the more industrial members of the CACM.

In addition to the increasing interregional trade deficits experienced by Honduras and Nicaragua, all five CACM members began to experience overall deteriorating terms of trade in the mid-1960's (see Table 3). While prices for traditional exports fell, imports from third countries, consisting in part of components used in the growing number of assembly plants, continued to rise. Deficits in the current accounts of the five members rose rapidly, and foreign capital inflows were insufficient to cover them.

Table 3

CURRENT ACCOUNTS IN THE BALANCE OF PAYMENTS OF THE
CENTRAL AMERICAN COUNTRIES, 1960-1967

(in millions of U.S. dollars)

	Guatemala	El Salvador	Honduras	Nicaragua	Costa Rica	TOTAL
1960	-25.9	-27.6	5.2	13.0	-18.9	-54.2
1961	-16.4	-0.3	5.0	-3.4	-13.8	-28.9
1962	-24.3	2.5	0.3	-9.7	-17.7	-48.9
1963	-30.6	-10.0	-13.9	-4.8	-25.4	-84.7
1964	-50.0	-23.3	-9.2	-9.1	-22.9	-114.5
1965	-49.7	-12.5	-5.7	-22.0	-67.2	-157.1
1966	-18.7	-41.0	-19.2	-49.1	-44.3	-172.3
1967	-66.4	-23.5	-28.5	-64.9	-50.2	-233.5

Sources: 1960, 1961: Computed from figures in Boletín Estadístico, Año I, No. 1 (Consejo Monetario Centroamericano, 1965), p. 106;
1962, 1963: Computed from figures in Boletín Estadístico, Año III, No. 3 (1966), p. 148;
1964, 1965: Boletín Estadístico, Año IV, No. 4 (1967), p. 150;
1966, 1967: Boletín Estadístico, Año V, No. 5 (1968), pp. 152-153.

This situation was aggravated by restrictions under which member governments found themselves as a consequence of the existence of the CACM. As one observer has noted, "National governments found that they had lost unilateral control over what had been a basic policy instrument for regulating the amount of imports and determining the quantity of fiscal revenue."[32] Whereas prior to the formation of the Common Market, a country could meet temporary balance-of-payments problems by limiting its imports of nonessential consumer items, after its formation an increasing percentage of these articles were imported from the rest of Central America, and were therefore no longer subject to restrictive measures. In addition, the construction of a common external tariff meant that CACM members could no longer unilaterally use the tariff as an instrument to regulate imports from third countries. Also, since integration had been somewhat successful in stimulating import substitution, there was increased demand for imports of semi-manufactures, capital goods, and raw materials--that is, inputs into manufacturing processes which governments were reluctant to restrict. The governments therefore found themselves in large part stripped of the primary and traditional instrument they had utilized to deal with imbalances. At the same time, the unwillingness of the five governments to regulate assembly industry activities created large import requirements which further increased balance-of-payments difficulties.

Each of the countries also began to face fiscal shortages by the mid-1960's.[33] In part this was a consequence of the policy of import substitution, which reduced tariffs on some items which yielded important revenues. (Such a policy would have a similar effect anywhere.) But these fiscal shortages were also a result of failure by the five countries to implement a common fiscal incentives agreement, and the subsequent attempts of each of them to offer greater tax and tariff concessions than the others-- another aspect of a reliance on unregulated market forces. This national competition sapped revenues from each of the governments. The weakening of the traditional primary source of income--duties from tariffs--occurred at the same time that demands for government expenditures, especially for public investment, increased. The need for significant revisions in national tax structures became evident, but no such revisions were made.

Therefore, by the mid-1960's the five Central American countries had freed trade and constructed a common tariff for most items, and by so doing, had stimulated an expansion of

---

[32]Schmitter, "The Process of CA Integration," pp. 20-21.

[33]See Hansen, Central America, pp. 81-84, for a discussion of fiscal problems in the region.

regional trade, a change in its composition, and an influx of industrial investment. But their reliance on unregulated market forces, as reflected in their inability to agree on and implement certain protocols, resulted in trading and investment patterns favoring the more developed over the less developed members. In addition, this reliance on the free operation of market forces appeared to exacerbate the fiscal and balance-of-payments problems of all of the governments, especially important after the favorable terms of trade enjoyed by the region's traditional exports began to deteriorate after 1964-1965.

Equality of Benefits: Political Considerations

As will be seen below, the tendency for unregulated market forces in Central America to increase disparities among member countries, once perceived by the less developed members in the region, became the source of a series of political crises in the CACM beginning in 1965. On the one side, the less developed members pressed for arrangements to ensure that they would receive benefits at least proportionate to the other members. On the other side, the more developed members, inhibited by limited resources in their pursuit of the goal of national economic growth, were reluctant to respond to the demands of their even less developed partners, and thereby sacrifice the present benefits they enjoyed from integration for uncertain future ones.

Neither the perceptions nor the initial behavior of the two groups of countries in the CACM should surprise us. In integration efforts among so-called underdeveloped countries, all national actors can be expected to be sensitive to any negative changes in the patterns of their economic transactions. When countries share economic development as one of their chief objectives and realize that their resources to accomplish it are severely limited--irrespective of their levels of development relative to one another--each of them can be expected to perceive changes in its economic transactions within the region of integration in terms of immediate benefits and (especially) costs to itself. Should a member country perceive that these changes are costly, it can be expected to press hard for benefits at least equal to those obtained by its partners; if the member believes it is not obtaining equitable benefits, it will threaten to and most likely will withdraw from the market unless an external source such as a foreign nation provides it with a sufficient payoff to remain inside. Those members who may be enjoying benefits, perceiving their overall resources as limited, can be expected to be extremely reluctant to forego them, even though this might lead to greater rewards in the future. They will be unwilling to respond to the complainant members in a way which satisfies the latter. In other words, in the context of general underdevelopment, bargaining over reciprocal benefits can be expected to be a controversial and difficult affair,[34] as has already been demonstrated in integration efforts in both Latin America and Africa.[35]

Nevertheless, it is precisely bargaining over reciprocal benefits which will be necessary if integration among underdeveloped countries is to proceed much beyond the mere freeing of trade and the construction of a common tariff. Reliance on the operation of market mechanisms within a protected free trade area perhaps will postpone the day of reckoning, but not for long. For it seems that in all common markets among underdeveloped countries, the operation of free market forces, when successful in stimulating growth in regional trade, import substitution, and increased investment, stimulates trading and investment patterns which, due to external economies, favor the traditional centers in the relatively more developed countries over the less developed members, even when initial differences in national levels of development are not severe. These changes in the patterns of regional trade also have fiscal consequences which appear to work against the less developed members. In that underdeveloped countries are highly sensitive to costs entailed by participation in integration, the controversial, not easily bargainable group of issues generally referred to as balanced development or unequal benefits, emerges to threaten the process of integration.

In addition, in the underdeveloped context, whether in Central America or in Africa, national balance-of-payments crises

---

[34]This is one of the primary empirical generalizations concerning integration efforts in the developing world set forth in Ernst Haas in "The Study of Regional Integration: Somber Reflections on the Joy and Anguish of Pre-Theorizing," International Organization, Summer 1970.

[35]For discussions of the emergence and significance of unequal benefits issues in integration efforts among underdeveloped countries, see Miguel Wionczek, "Introduction: Requisites for Viable Integration" in Wionczek, ed., Latin American Economic Integration: Experiences and Prospects (New York: Praeger, 1966), pp. 3-18; Sidney Dell, "The Early Years of LAFTA" in ibid., esp. pp. 108-115; Hansen, Central America, esp. pp. 56-64, and "Regional Integration: Reflections on a Decade of Theoretical Efforts," World Politics, Vol. XXI, No. 2 (January 1969), pp. 242-271; Joseph Nye, "Patterns and Catalysts in Regional Integration" in J. Nye, International Regionalism, pp. 333-349; Abdul A. Jalloh, "Neo-Functionalism and Regional Political Integration in Africa" (Yale University, 1970; unpublished); Aaron Segal, "The Integration of Developing Countries: Some Thoughts on East Africa and Central America," Journal of Common Market Studies, Vol. V, No. 3 (March 1967), pp. 252-282.

may be perceived as an unequal benefits issue. Given the dependence of the underdeveloped countries on a few exports for which world prices fluctuate greatly, such crises are fairly common occurrences. Yet, one of the consequences of the formation of a common market is that countries find themselves without the old and tried instrument used to alleviate temporary balance-of-payments problems--i.e., restrictions on imports of nonessential consumer items. On the other hand, cutbacks by a less developed member of "heavy" imports from third countries might undermine its economic growth and place it in a disadvantageous position relative to other common market members.

It is the emergence and resolution of just such a series of highly controversial issues as that of balanced development or unequal benefits which for neo-functionalist integration theorists provides a test for determining whether national actors will upgrade or downgrade the scope and/or level of their commitment to mutual decision-making.[36] Given the controversiality of this set of issues and the fact that it appears generally (and perhaps even inevitably) to emerge and to threaten all integration efforts by underdeveloped countries, the resolution of such conflicts provides probably the most salient test for determining whether a common market among such countries will spill over or spill back. With this in mind, I will first describe each of the crises over balanced development which has taken place in the CACM. Then, I will analyze the conflicts in terms of what they indicate about the types of learning and patterns of mutual responsiveness which have occurred in the region. Finally, I will discuss the extent to which actor-learning and patterns of responsiveness in Central America have resulted in and can be expected in the near future to result in spill-over or spill-back.

---

[36] See the discussion of politicization in Ernst B. Haas and Philippe C. Schmitter, "Economics and Differential Patterns of Political Integration: Projections about Unity in Latin America," International Organization, Vol. XVIII, No. 4 (August 1964), and Schmitter, "Three Neo-Functional Hypotheses about International Integration," International Organization, Vol. XXIII, No. 1 (Winter 1969), pp. 161-166. [The Haas-Schmitter article is also in H. Bull et al., International Political Communities: An Anthology (New York: Doubleday, 1966)]. For Haas and Schmitter, politicization constitutes "one of the properties of integration--the intervening variable between economic and political integration. . . ." Schmitter holds that "the minimal threshold for politicization [of an integration effort] is a rise in the controversiality of the regional decision-making process." The process of politicization as a whole includes, in addition, a widening of the clientele involved in integration, a redefinition and transcendence of the original goals, and a shift in actor expectations and loyalties toward the new regional center.

II. UNEQUAL BENEFITS: HONDURAS' DEMAND FOR PREFERENTIAL TREATMENT

Prior to 1964, there is no conclusive evidence that Honduran decision-makers perceived the pattern of economic transactions in the Central American region to be especially unfavorable. Two events--one economic and the other political--changed that. First, Honduras experienced its first regional trade deficit in 1963, and the deficit grew worse in 1964; second, the Liberal government, which had been favorable to the CACM and had entered it without seeking much in the way of special help, was ousted by a coup in 1963.[1]

Although the ouster of the Liberal government in itself was unrelated to the country's role in the Common Market, it helped set the stage for a shift in Honduras' perception of and policy toward the market. In contrast to the Liberals, the post-1963 government, upon attaining power, had no definite position on the Common Market. But some of the new economic officials perceived Honduras' position in the CACM as disadvantageous. They began to press the government to demand treaty revisions in Honduras' favor. The initial demand that the Honduran government seek preferential treatment from the more developed members was made by Práxedes Martínez, Sub-Secretary of the Ministry of Economy during the provisional military government, and later Economic Advisor to the National Congress. Beginning in 1964 Martínez pressed the government to act through speeches to business groups, magazine articles, and discussions with other government officials. His influential position in the legislature after 1965 meant that

---

[1]The Liberal government of Honduras had not deposited the Common Fiscal Incentives Agreement prior to its overthrow in October 1963, but the author has been unable to uncover any evidence that it had not done so because it wanted to press for revisions in the agreement. Given the absence of such evidence, the Liberal government's general support for integration, and the fact that a one-year delay in deposits was usual rather than exceptional, it would appear that the Liberal government's failure to deposit was due to other factors--perhaps only the commonplace administrative delay which characterized that country. In fact, at the time of the coup in Honduras, only Guatemala (June 14, 1963) and Costa Rica (September 23, 1963) had deposited the agreement. El Salvador did not deposit it until February 14, 1964, and Nicaragua not until February 1, 1965.

the government could expect a fight over passage of any integration agreement.[2]

Martínez claimed that the previous government had made several errors in negotiating the General Treaty because it had not taken account of Honduras' weakness relative to the other member states.[3] According to Martínez, Honduras, compared to the other Common Market members, suffered from low industrial production, a deficiency in electrical energy output, a poor highway network, low technical skills, and political instability. As a result of these disadvantages, it should not have been expected to compete favorably with the rest of the Common Market countries. And it had not done so. He claimed that as a result of its backwardness and of entering the CACM without seeking special treatment, Honduras' economic position had declined: its regional trade balance had become unfavorable, its regional terms of trade were deteriorating, its consumer prices were rising, and the number of its unemployed artisans was growing as a result of industrial competition from the other Common Market members. Finally, he charged that Honduras was suffering from diminished fiscal revenues as a result of the exportation by the more developed members of the CACM of their pseudo-Central American products to Honduras exempt from tariffs; Honduras was in effect subsidizing the industrial development of the other Central American states. It was so backward that it could not even satisfy the conditions to obtain integration industries which might help it to industrialize.

According to Martínez, what the previous government neglected to demand, and what Honduras needed, was preferential treatment to help it adapt to the new market conditions: a grace period for the application of the uniform tariff, a protocol to the Central American Common Fiscal Incentives Agreement to be negotiated before Honduras' deposit which would provide extra exemptions and benefits to firms in order to attract industry, and the creation of a development fund to transfer capital to areas as compensation for the absorption of its market by the other CACM members. Without special treatment, Honduras would fall further behind the rest of the Common Market countries.

Martínez not only wrote articles and made direct efforts to convince government officials of his arguments, but he also worked closely with private groups to advance his views. He

---

[2]Interview with Guillermo Bueso, Chief of the Department of Economic Studies, Central Bank of Honduras, August 1966.

[3]For Martínez' position, see especially his article in La Industria, organ of the National Industrial Association of Honduras, November 1964, pp. 3-10.

helped the National Association of Industrialists (ANDI) draft
an open letter to the Minister of Economy in which they requested
that the minister press for preferential treatment from the other
CACM members.[4] The argument, claims, and demands were those of
Martínez. The letter listed Honduras' deficiencies and claimed
that its regional economic transactions had deteriorated since
the formation of the Common Market. Corrective measures suggested
included all those previously recommended by Martínez plus the
renegotiation of common tariffs on all articles newly traded in
the region since 1959. In the event that the other Common Market
members refused to adopt these corrective measures, the ANDI note
threatened that "we would seriously consider the declaration of
a halt in the deposit of new integration instruments in those
areas affecting the surrender of markets and fiscal losses." Both
Martínez' articles and speeches and the industrialists' letter
noted that the country's low growth rate was not due entirely to
the Common Market, but also reflected a lack of aggressiveness
on the part of the public sector. The charge was made that the
government's investments in infrastructure were low and, because
of extreme administrative disorganization, it had granted almost
no fiscal incentives to industry.

In his reply to the letter from ANDI, the Minister of
Economy promised that he would seek the opinions of other national sectors on the Common Market, and then appoint a governmental
commission to adivse him regarding the advantages of continuing,
with or without adjustments, in the Program of Economic Integration.[5] In addition, the minister sent the ANDI note to SIECA
for its comments.[6]

---

[4] ANDI, Nota No. 949, 3 de diciembre de 1964; mimeo. Martínez'
role in the drafting was confirmed in an interview with Martínez,
December 1965.

[5] Letter sent by Minister of Economy to President of ANDI:
Secretaría de Economía y Hacienda, República de Honduras, Nota
No. 255, 10 de diciembre de 1964; mimeo.

[6] Letter sent by Minister of Economy to Secretary-General of
SIECA: Secretaría de Economía y Hacienda, República de Honduras,
Nota No. 356, 10 de diciembre de 1964; mimeo. SIECA did not com-
ment on ANDI's claims for eight months. Finally, in August 1965,
the Secretary-General of SIECA sent a detailed reply to the minister in which SIECA rejected the charges made by ANDI. In doing
so, it used very selected figures, largely ignoring data which
might offer contrary evidence (Letter from Pedro Abelardo Delgado,
Secretary-General, SIECA, to Minister of Economy, Honduras, August
2, 1965; mimeo. Enclosed with the letter was the more detailed
reply by SIECA entitled "Comentarios de la SIECA al pronunciamiento

By the end of 1964, Martínez' strategy appeared to be succeeding. Criticisms in the press of the country's disadvantageous position in the CACM were common. As a result of the criticisms, especially that of Martínez, who after all was a government official, rumors of Honduras' possible withdrawal from the Common Market spread within Honduras and abroad, although neither Martínez nor ANDI advocated such a policy. Criticism and rumors grew to the extent that the Military Head of Government in his New Year's Message of 1965 felt the need to clarify the government's position.[7] Although he reiterated the government's support for the CACM and declared that "instigation from certain sectors toward having Honduras withdraw from the integration treaties is completely contrary to the economic policy of the Military Government," he also indicated that Honduras might require special treatment.[8]

Criticisms of the country's policy with regard to regional integration did not subside during 1965, despite the fact that Honduras was enjoying a high overall growth rate due to an expansion in its agricultural exports to third countries.[9] In fact, the national official most directly concerned with integration policy lent support to the critics' views. The newly appointed Minister of Economy appeared to agree with the national critics of the CACM, and used their arguments in regional negotiations. Although Central Bank officials cautioned him that portraying Honduras as backward in order to obtain concessions from the other four countries might have a boomerang effect and frighten away potential investors, the minister disregarded their advice.[10] During his first months in office, the new minister began to develop a more aggressive policy toward the Common Market; this became most evident with regard to Honduras' stand on national and regional fiscal incentives.

---

de la Asociación Nacional de Industriales de Honduras"). There is no indication that SIECA's late reply influenced either ANDI or the minister.

[7] See SIECA, Carta Informativa, No. 39, for the comments made by the Honduran Head of Government.

[8] This is the interpretation given to the statement in U.S. Department of State, American Embassy, Honduras, "Economic Survey," Fourth Quarter, 1964, p. 9.

[9] See ECLA (Economic Commission for Latin America), Economic Survey of Latin America 1965 (E/CN.12/752/Rev. 1), pp. 185-192, for an analysis of the Honduran economy in 1965.

[10] Interview with Bueso.

HONDURAS' DEMAND FOR PREFERENTIAL TREATMENT

After the five Central American countries signed the Common Fiscal Incentives Agreement on July 31, 1962, SIECA in 1963 prepared draft bylaws to the protocol for consideration by the Executive Council.[11] During 1964 and early 1965 negotiations over the bylaws within the council proceeded slowly, but apparently with some success. During its meetings in January and March 1965, the council routinely approved several of the articles.[12] But by early October there were two indications that discussions over the regulations would come to naught--that the Honduran government did not intend to deposit the original agreement without revisions favorable to it, and that it would follow a generally more aggressive policy in the Common Market.

First, the new Honduran Minister of Economy seemed more committed to national industrial development than his predecessors had been. During his first months in office he granted many more concessions to industries than the previous minister had over a much longer period. More significant, there was a new industrial incentives law before the National Congress which, if implemented, would allow the minister to grant greater benefits to firms than those in effect in the rest of the region. There was no indication that he planned to abandon this proposal, designed to allow Honduras to catch up with the more developed members, in favor of uniform fiscal incentives.

The second indication of a more aggressive Honduran position was a newspaper interview given by the minister in October. Basing his argument on a study carried out in the ministry, he claimed that "inequality in levels of development" between Honduras and the other CACM members had been "accentuated as a direct result of the formation of the Common Market," and that although "Honduras is in the best disposition to continue within the framework of economic integration," it "is fully convinced of the necessity of putting into effect the principle of balanced development."[13] As evidence of the accentuated inequality, the minister noted that: (1) the other Common Market countries enjoyed annual growth rates of up to 6 percent, in contrast to the Honduran average of 4 percent; (2) along with its low economic growth rate, Honduras had the highest rate of population growth, with the exception of Costa Rica; and (3) as a result of the greater dynamism of the economies of the other members, Honduras' traditional surplus in regional trade had become a deficit.

---

[11] SIECA, Carta Informativa, No. 28, p. 6.

[12] SIECA, Carta Informativa, No. 40, p. 4; No. 41, p. 3.

[13] El Día (Tegucigalpa), 25 October 1965, p. 12.

The tougher Honduran policy was demonstrated in late October when the Honduran delegate, in Executive Council discussions of the bylaws to the protocol, expressed his government's concern over possible unfavorable effects on his country of a uniform reclassification of industries.[14] Since this "concern," at the very least, signified continued non-deposit and a probable request for revision, the council turned the issue of fiscal incentives over to the Economic Council for resolution.

Of the discussion on fiscal incentives that took place at the next meeting of the Economic Council, held in November, the Secretariat reported in its newsletter that "in view of the declaration made by the Minister of Honduras," "in light of proposals made by [Honduras]," and "in order to adapt said agreement to the requirements of industrial development," the council decided to call an Extraordinary Meeting in a few months to examine the provisions of the Fiscal Incentives Agreement.[15] It appears that the minister's "declaration" was to the effect that Honduras viewed the instrument as it stood to be prejudicial to Honduras, and would not deposit it until it was revised. This interpretation is supported by a statement made by the Honduran minister only a short time later:

> The Government of Honduras believes that the ratification of this Convention would add to the unfavorable effects on the Honduran economy observed between 1958 and 1965, and certain clauses of the Convention would clearly retard and lessen the possibilities of the industrial growth of Honduras in the short, medium and long terms.[16]

With regard to revisions, the minister at this point asked only for preferential treatment in general terms. He had not yet decided on specific requests.[17]

At the same time as this controversy was developing, the Secretariat of the Economic Commission for Latin America (ECLA), the initial stimulator of Central American integration in the 1950's, was preparing a report on the progress of the CACM to be

---

[14]SIECA, Carta Informativa, No. 49, p. 16.

[15]Ibid., p. 11.

[16]"Exposition of Honduras Regarding the Central American Convention on Fiscal Incentives to Industrial Development," 11 January 1966, in Wardlaw, p. 90.

[17]Interview with Armando O. Valladeres, Office of Economic Integration, Honduran Ministry of Economy, August 1966.

presented to the Ninth Meeting of its Committee on Economic Co-operation (CCE), which consisted of the five Central American Ministers of Economy, to be held in January 1966. For several months prior to the meeting, ECLA officials had consulted regional officials in order to take into account all the problems and conditions relating to the process of integration.[18] As part of its task of investigating the important problems facing the Common Market and bringing them to the attention of the CCE, the ECLA Secretariat investigated the economic position of Honduras relative to the other countries in the region. In the document it presented to the CCE it concluded that although all five countries had benefited from integration and had been stimulated by the Common Market, an imbalance in levels of development and rates of growth unfavorable to Honduras continued to exist.[19] It recommended several measures to ensure a more reasonable balance between Honduras' industrial development and that in the rest of the region. Honduras presented to the CCE its own study, carried out in its Ministry of Economy, which emphasized to an even greater extent than the ECLA document its need for preferential treatment to fulfill the principle of balanced development.[20]

Based on ECLA's suggestions, the Central American Ministers of Economy in their role as the CCE recommended to the Economic Council that it grant several types of preferential treatment to Honduras. They recommended (1) that the council draw up a list of those industries eligible for integration industry status and Special System status[21] and carry out technical studies

---

[18] SIECA, Carta Informativa, No. 52, p. 2.

[19] "El crecimiento económico de Honduras y el desarrollo equilibrado en la integración centroamericana" (CEPAL E/CN/12/762), p. 200.

[20] "Exposición sobre la participación de Honduras en el proceso de integración económica centroamericana" (CCE/IX/D.T.2).

[21] El Salvador proposed a Special System for the Promotion of Productive Activities in 1963. The System was approved by the Economic Council and is applied through protocols ratified and deposited by national governments. Under its provisions, additional tariff protection may be granted to firms producing goods previously not manufactured in the region, and capable of supplying at least 50 percent of the region's demand. The System was attached to the first Protocol on Integration Industries, in part to mitigate Salvadorean opposition. Unlike the integration industries scheme, it does not deal with the problem of balanced development, and its operation may lead to even greater imbalances. The System has been popular, with the Executive Council routinely processing requests, which are later attached to protocols.

to determine which industries should be assigned to Honduras to accelerate its industrial development, (2) that CABEI grant priority to Honduran projects, (3) that Honduras receive special treatment from international lending and technical institutions, (4) that ICAITI, ESAPAC, and other regional organs help formulate specific programs for Honduras, and (5) that Honduras be granted preferences in the concession of fiscal incentives through the adoption of a protocol to the Common Fiscal Incentives Agreement. In exchange for this special treatment, the CCE asked Honduras to ratify and deposit its outstanding integration agreements.[22]

In sum, the ministers sitting as the CCE recognized the existence of the problem of imbalance, basically accepted the Honduran interpretation that the term "balanced development" referred to balanced _industrial_ development, and agreed that Honduras merited several forms of preferential treatment. Moreover, there appears to have been little disagreement about most of the recommendations suggested by the ECLA Secretariat and passed by the CCE. This is understandable: from its founding CABEI had granted priority to Honduran projects; special treatment by other regional and international agencies probably was not viewed as of great significance by the other four countries; and feasibility studies of possible integration industries would not solve the basic problem of attracting capital to the integration industries scheme and to Honduras--i.e., feasibility studies did not mean the actual establishment of industries. Most important to Honduras was the CCE recommendation of a preferential system of fiscal incentives to attract additional industrial investment. The CCE did not specify the content of this system, but left that to be worked out by the Economic Council. Ominously, the recommendation by the CCE of special treatment for Honduras stimulated the Nicaraguan delegation to request that its position within the Common Market also be studied; the committee recommended that a working group in SIECA be established for that purpose.[23]

On the day following the CCE meeting, the ministers reconstituted themselves as the Central American Economic Council and held the Extraordinary Meeting called for in the previous November. In light of the Honduran refusal to deposit the Common Fiscal Incentives Agreement, the council accepted the CCE [its own] recommendations.[24] It charged ICAITI and SIECA with studying which integration industries might be established in

---

[22]See CCE, Res. 141, SIECA, _Carta Informativa_, No. 52, pp. 16-17.

[23]See CCE, Res. 142, _ibid._, p. 17.

[24]Economic Council, Res. 23, _ibid._, p. 21.

Honduras,[25] and SIECA with drafting the necessary protocol to the Common Fiscal Incentives Agreement in time for the next council meeting in April.[26]

Initial implementation of the resolution regarding integration industries proceeded smoothly. Honduras quickly named a National Commission of Industrial Development which met with representatives of SIECA and ICAITI twice, in February and March 1966. These regional and national officials agreed to elaborate an inventory of basic data about industries of possible regional interest, and then determined which industries should be studied. These studies were to provide the basis for decisions by the Economic Council for inclusion under integration industry status or under the Special System. In July, an Ad Hoc Inter-Institutional Commission, consisting of the heads of ICAITI, SIECA, JOPLAN, and CABEI, was formed to carry out the studies.[27]

The primary bone of contention was what extra fiscal incentives the other members were willing to offer Honduras. The first major clash over the issue took place at the April meeting of the Economic Council.[28] SIECA presented its proposal to give Honduras the right to import raw materials and machinery for its industries exempt from tariffs, and to allow it to grant tax exemptions for a period of time longer than that allowed for the other four countries. The four ministers agreed to the extension of the tax benefits, but they rejected the proposed free import of raw materials, claiming that such an advantage would destroy competition in the region.

At this point, El Salvador suggested that the four members grant Honduras a 20 percent-plus differential on the import of raw materials for its new industries. Although Guatemala, Costa Rica, and Nicaragua agreed to the Salvadorean proposal, there was disagreement concerning when the differential would begin. Honduras wanted it to be effective immediately upon the implementation of the Common Fiscal Incentives Agreement; the others, beginning with the sixth year of the agreement.

---

[25] Economic Council, Res. 24, ibid., pp. 21-22.

[26] Economic Council, Res. 25, ibid., p. 22.

[27] SIECA, Carta Informativa, No. 57, p. 10.

[28] The minutes of the April meeting are unavailable to the author. What follows is a reconstruction of events based largely on an interview with Guillermo Noriega Morales, Director, Department of Industrial Affairs, SIECA, Guatemala City, September 1966.

Both sides had good reasons for their positions. According to the basic Common Fiscal Incentives Agreement, industries were to be classified by national criteria for the first seven years, then by regional criteria. If Honduras were granted a 20 percent differential for new industries to be effective beginning with the sixth year of the agreement, it would enjoy substantially less of an advantage than if the differential were effective beginning with the first year. If it became effective in the sixth year, Honduras would be able to classify industries as "new" according to national criteria for only two years; then it would have to adopt regional criteria of classification. This would be highly disadvantageous for Honduras, and would reduce tremendously the preferential effect of the proposed differential. In addition, to delay the implementation until the sixth year would mean that the more developed members would not lose any of their advantage during the period in which the greatest benefits would be granted-- the first five years.[29] A delay in the effective date, therefore, was highly unfavorable to Honduras and favorable to the other four members.

Finally, in addition to the proposed exemptions from tariffs and extended tax exemptions, Honduras requested that a different, preferential system of industrial classification be applied to it than was applied to the other four members. This was rejected outright by the four others. It would have undermined the entire fiscal incentives framework.

After it became clear that there would be no agreement on which fiscal incentives preferences to grant Honduras, the council asked SIECA to prepare a document in which it set forth, on the one hand, the positions taken by the four members on the Salvadorean proposal and, on the other hand, the position taken by Honduras, and to make a new proposal taking these conflicting positions into account.

Almost simultaneously with the Economic Council meeting, representatives of ANDI proposed that the Central American Industrial Federation (FECAICA) support the Honduran request for

---

[29] According to the Common Fiscal Incentives Agreement, companies classified as Group A new industries receive a 100 percent exemption from customs duties on the import of raw materials for the first five years, 60 percent during the next three years, and 40 percent during the next two years (Central American Agreement on Fiscal Incentives, Article XI). If the Honduran demand that the differential begin immediately were granted, Honduras would receive the 100 percent exemption for the first five years, while the other countries would receive only an 80 percent exemption.

preferential treatment.[30] FECAICA rejected the ANDI request and remained opposed to special treatment for Honduras--especially tariff exemptions on the import of raw materials--throughout the year.

By the time of the next scheduled meeting of the Executive and Economic Councils in June, SIECA had prepared only a document which set forth the positions of Honduras and the other members on the Salvadorean proposal.[31] It appears that it had been unable to reach agreement on any new proposal. In fact, since April each country had prepared an independent request for the reform of the Common Fiscal Incentives Agreement.

To protest the lack of responsiveness by other members and to press its demands, Honduras adopted a new tactic. Previously it refused only to deposit the Common Fiscal Incentives Agreement. Now it boycotted the meetings of both councils. As a result, neither the Executive nor the Economic Council could hold its meetings. In light of this unprecedented crisis, SIECA officials urged the other ministers to concentrate on resolving the immediate problem before pressing their own requests for reform of the Common Fiscal Incentives Agreement.[32]

The only common thread in the requests by other Common Market members was that each was addressed to the special problem of the proposing country. The Guatemalan minister, although accepting the idea of the Salvadorean proposal, was preparing to ask that the 20 percent differential be made applicable to industries which established themselves in underdeveloped areas of the other member countries. The Executive Council would rule on the eligibility of areas.[33] Guatemala presumably would benefit most from this proposal, given its underdeveloped, Indian-populated interior.

Nicaragua intended to demand preferences identical to those Honduras would receive. Although its diminished rate of growth in 1965 (the result of a fall in the price of cotton), its worsening regional trade deficit, and its forthcoming elections seemed

---

[30] Interview with Augusto Barán Lupán, Vice Manager, ANDI, Tegucigalpa, September 1966.

[31] Interview with Noriega Morales.

[32] Ibid.

[33] Interview with Carlos Enrique Gutiérrez Luna, Director, Department of Economic Integration, Ministry of Economy, Guatemala, September 1966.

to stimulate the Nicaraguan demand, it is doubtful that Nicaragua would have requested special treatment had not Honduras done so. Only after it appeared that Honduras would receive preferences did Nicaraguan officials prepare a report for presentation to the Economic Council which attempted to demonstrate that on the basis of its economic position Nicaragua also needed preferential treatment.[34]

Finally, Costa Rica was preparing to request a restructuring of the entire fiscal incentives framework. It wanted to abolish all tariff exemptions as incentives, and then formulate other types of preferences to assist Honduras.[35] By abolishing tariff exemptions, Costa Rica hoped to increase its revenues and thereby relieve its fiscal shortages as well as to alleviate its balance-of-payments difficulties.

In meetings with national economic officials urging them to focus on the immediate problem, SIECA officials reported on the results of an analysis made by the Secretariat concerning the possible consequences for the other four countries should they adopt the differential favoring Honduras. SIECA's analysis concluded that overall cost differentials would increase by not more than 1.5 percent. At almost the same time, the Guatemalan Ministry of Economy carried out a similar study with similar results.[36]

In the context of a Common Market whose chief organs had been stagnating since April 1966, and in light of SIECA's analysis and urgings, momentum seemed to develop for a resolution of the crisis. At the meeting of the Economic Council called by SIECA to finally resolve the issue, SIECA prevailed in its argument that the Honduran requests be dealt with on the basis of previous proposals and before detailed consideration was given to alternative suggestions. As a result, the Guatemalans did not bring up their request, and the Costa Rican proposal was shelved for later consideration. Nicaragua, however, pursued its request that it be granted preferential treatment and, to justify its case, presented a document entitled "Effects of the CACM on the Nicaraguan Economy." The Salvadorean Minister of Economy flatly rejected the Nicaraguan request. One of the most knowledgeable observers of the CACM claims that the Nicaraguan minister threatened withdrawal from the CACM if Nicaragua's request for

---

[34] Interviews with officials in Nicaraguan Ministry of Economy, August 1966.

[35] SIECA, Carta Informativa, No. 60, pp. 11-12.

[36] Interview with Gutiérrez Luna.

preferential treatment was not granted, and that the Salvadorean minister threatened withdrawal if it was.[37] But the council decided that a procedure similar to that previously applied to the Honduran request would be followed in Nicaragua's case as well. ECLA would study the relative position of Nicaragua in the CACM, and on the basis of that study the CCE would make pertinent recommendations to the Economic Council.[38] Nicaragua agreed to this procedure.

With other proposals shelved for the moment, the council agreed that Honduras would be able to grant 20 percent more in tariff exemptions for the import of raw materials and semi-manufactures than the other Common Market members to new industries falling into Groups A and B.[39] These exemptions were to become effective upon implementation of the basic agreement and this protocol. In addition, the council decided to allow Honduras the right to grant to new and existing industries in Groups A and C, as well as to new industries in Group B, exemptions from tariffs on the import of machinery and exemptions from taxes on income and assets for two years longer than the other Central American countries. It was also allowed to grant to existing industries in Group B an additional year of exemptions from tariffs on the import of machinery, two extra years of income tax exemptions, and three additional years of exemptions from taxes on assets.[40] These preferences were far greater than those offered to Honduras under the original agreement. In that agreement it received the right merely to grant new industries in

---

[37]Hansen, Central America, p. 46.

[38]See Economic Council, Res. 29, SIECA, Carta Informativa, No. 60, p. 8.

[39]Under the Common Fiscal Incentives Agreement, signed in 1962, industrial operations are classified into three main categories: Group A consists of producers of industrial raw materials, capital goods, and--if made up of 50 percent Central American raw materials--consumer goods, containers, or semi-manufactures; Group B consists of producers of other consumer goods, containers, or semi-manufactures which improve the balance-of-payments situation and include a high added value in their manufacture; Group C consists of other industries, including assembling and packaging. Industries in each category are also classified as "new" or "existing" firms. "New" firms in Group A are eligible for the maximum benefits offered, and "existing" firms in Group C for the minimum.

[40]See Economic Council, Res. 28, SIECA, Carta Informativa, No. 60, p. 7.

Groups A and B exemptions from taxes on income and assets for two extra years.

The Protocol for Preferential Treatment for Honduras was signed by the Ministers of Economy in September 1966, but the four other members, and especially El Salvador, were slow to ratify and deposit it.[41] Most deposits were made only under great political pressures. Honduras ratified both the basic agreement and the protocol in December 1967, but used its continued refusal to deposit the basic agreement as a weapon with which to force the others to deposit the preferential treatment protocol. But, as indicated below, deposit by El Salvador occurred only after even greater political pressures were used. The agreement did not become legally effective until March 1969. In practice, it still (July 1970) remains inoperative.

The Nicaraguan request for special treatment remains under ECLA study nearly four years after referral. ECLA appears in no hurry to report on it. This delay in bringing the issue to the attention of the Ministers of Economy either in their role as the CCE or as the Economic Council is probably due to ECLA's awareness of the opposition of most of the Common Market members, and especially El Salvador, to preferential treatment for Nicaragua, and its fear that the reopening of the issue almost certainly would create another crisis.

---

[41]The dates of deposit were as follows: Nicaragua--September 1967, Costa Rica--June 1968, Guatemala--October 1968, El Salvador--March 1969, Honduras--March 1969. Honduras deposited the Preferential Treatment Protocol and the Common Fiscal Incentives Agreement on the same day El Salvador deposited the protocol.

III. NATIONAL BALANCE-OF-PAYMENTS DIFFICULTIES
AND FISCAL SHORTAGES: COSTA RICA

As indicated above, reliance on the operation of unregulated market forces in the context of a protected free trade area
intensified strains on both the balance-of-payments and fiscal
situations of all CACM members. Although favorable world markets
for the region's exports in the early 1960's mitigated these pressures, large deficits developed in the overall current accounts
of Costa Rica, the most liberal of the member countries in granting industrial concessions, and of Guatemala, with a somewhat
similar policy. Guatemala's current accounts deficit almost
doubled between 1963 and 1964. Its tax revenues as a percentage
of gross national product had declined steadily since 1961, its
public savings had dropped, and the government had borrowed heavily abroad.[1] Costa Rica also had been pressed fiscally and had
been forced to borrow abroad. Nicaragua, which had had the highest customs duties in the region prior to the implementation of
the common tariff, had imposed consumption taxes on several items
to relieve fiscal pressures. In Honduras, Práxedes Martínez was
demanding preferential treatment based in part on the argument
that, as a consequence of freely traded regional products, Honduras was losing receipts from tariffs which diminished its capacity to finance development programs.

By 1964, officials in several Ministries of Economy appeared concerned about what they held to be, at least in part,
the adverse effects of the regional policy of import substitution. In this context the Guatemalan Minister of Economy proposed to the Economic Council in June that it hold a joint meeting with the Ministers of Finance to discuss their fiscal problems.[2] The council agreed and asked SIECA to make the necessary
contacts and prepare the agenda for a meeting scheduled for
November.

SIECA delayed calling the joint meeting, however, so that
it would be able to benefit from the conclusions of the still
uncompleted Inter-American Development Bank/Organization of American States (IDB/OAS) Joint Taxation Program study of Central

---

[1] For a discussion of the Guatemalan economic situation, see
Hansen, Central America, pp. 81 and 84.

[2] SIECA, Carta Informativa, No. 33, p. 7.

American fiscal systems, as well as from a memo on tax reform it requested from the Pan American Union.[3] The Economic Council in early 1965 decided to expand the scope of the meeting and discuss fiscal problems within the wider framework of regional development policy.[4] In the meantime, the Guatemalan Ministers of Economy and Finance declared that they would seek regional solutions to alleviate their country's serious balance-of-payments deficit, and El Salvador, in order to slow down the deterioration of its commercial balance, restricted bank credit for financing imports.[5] When SIECA finally called the joint meeting for April 1965, there appears to have been widespread concern about the effects of integration on government revenues and on rising import bills throughout the area, as well as some feeling that regional action was necessary.

SIECA's preparations were extensive. It organized the April meeting around both its own reports and recommendations and those of other regional organizations.[6] A resume of the IDB/OAS taxation study and a SIECA note served as the basis for discussions and resolutions on fiscal policy; a statement by the Monetary Council and ideas adopted at the first meeting of the region's planning directors (called by SIECA) were sources of recommendations to alleviate balance-of-payments difficulties; and the conclusions of the planning directors also served as the basis for resolutions on regional planning, foreign trade, and foreign investment policies.

With regard to fiscal policy, the delegates asked an Advisory Committee--consisting of representatives from SIECA, the Joint Planning Mission, and the Joint Taxation Program--to carry out a study of a program of harmonization of the Central American fiscal systems. But most of the resolutions passed at the April meeting focused on balance-of-payments difficulties. To help put a halt to the deterioration of their balance-of-payments situations, the ministers suggested a variety of measures. They supported continued use of monetary, exchange, and credit

---

[3] Report on the First Joint Meeting in La Industria (Tegucigalpa), July 1965, pp. 20-23.

[4] SIECA, Carta Informativa, No. 40, pp. 14-15.

[5] "Economic Survey," U.S. Department of State, American Embassy, Guatemala, First Quarter 1965 [mimeo]; "Summary of Economic Conditions," U.S. Department of State, American Embassy, El Salvador, First Quarter 1965 [mimeo].

[6] For details of the meeting, see SIECA, Carta Informativa, No. 42, pp. 13-19.

measures by the Central Banks, but urged them to coordinate their activities at the regional level. They asked SIECA and the Monetary Council to study exchange regulations on capital movements, the regulation of external financing by suppliers, and the imposition of consumer taxes on nonessentials. Finally, the delegates asked SIECA to prepare the draft of a protocol to provide for a more flexible system of tariff renegotiation for use as an instrument of development. Perhaps most important in the long run, the two sets of ministers institutionalized their meeting and appointed SIECA as their Executive Secretariat. By this action, the Ministers of Economy confirmed their right to deal with balance-of-payments and fiscal issues at the regional level, brought the Ministers of Finance into the integration nexus, and helped ensure that a regional point of view and continuity of action would pervade future meetings.

During the year following the April meeting there was no regional action on either balance-of-payments or fiscal problems, even though both remained serious. In fact, the trade deficits of Costa Rica and Guatemala increased alarmingly during 1965. The lack of regional activity appears to have been largely a consequence of the general crisis in the CACM created by Honduras' demand for preferential treatment, and by its boycott of regional meetings. In responding to that crisis, regional authorities had no time to deal with less important issues.[7] And neither Costa Rica nor Guatemala appeared willing to raise either issue in a way which would threaten the Common Market.

By late 1966, however, the situation had changed. On the one hand, the Honduran demand had been dealt with, at least temporarily, and regional meetings had been resumed. On the other hand, Costa Rica had a new government which found itself in an economic crisis.[8] The government's major problem was a severe shortage of foreign exchange caused by trade deficits, which had amounted to nearly U.S.$200 million since 1961. The trade deficits were in large part a consequence of the disastrous effects on agricultural production of the eruption of the Irazu volcano. But the deficits were also a result of the previous government's liberal application of the industrial development

---

[7] Interview with Eduardo Bolanos, Head of Department of Information, SIECA, August 1966.

[8] Aspects of the Costa Rica economic crisis are dealt with in Banco Central de Costa Rica, Memoria anual: 1967--La economía nacional (San José, 1968), pp. 36-40; Hansen, Central America, pp. 85-88; First National City Bank of New York, Foreign Information Service, "A Progress Report: The Central American Common Market" (New York, June 1967), p. 13.

law. This policy had stimulated assemblage activities involving
little value added. It also had led to increased domestic consumption of nonessential items. Revenues from tariffs had been
undermined, and continued heavy government expenditures on social
and economic development programs had further aggravated the fiscal situation. Measures adopted by the previous government to
meet the fiscal crisis had only intensified the problem. The government had taken out several short-term loans at home and abroad,
and the new government faced a situation in which amortization of
these loans increased the drain on foreign exchange reserves. In
addition, between 1959 and 1966 the Central Bank expanded the
money supply by 40 percent, which had contributed to a weakening
of the country's balance-of-payments situation.

Confronted with an increasingly severe foreign exchange
shortage, pressure from the International Monetary Fund, and an
unimproved fiscal situation, the new government devised a new
economic policy. First, it tightened credit conditions. Then
late in 1966, for the first time in many years, it proposed to
the national legislature a balanced budget balanced by new taxes--
5 percent land and sales taxes, increased excise taxes on cars,
and new excise taxes on several items. But the opposition-controlled National Assembly rejected the government's budget proposals.

In light of this rejection, Central Bank officials drafted
an austerity program designed to increase revenues and cut imports
The program included a temporary multiple exchange system which
discriminated against the import of nonessentials. This was to
be effective until passage by the Assembly of a bill authorizing
the bank to levy foreign exchange surcharges. The bank passed
the measure to the Executive, which in January 1967 imposed the
multiple exchange system by decree and introduced the bill regarding surcharges to the Assembly. Both measures applied to imports from all countries, including CACM members.

Reaction from regional authorities and economic officials
from the other four CACM members was quick, uniform, and decisive.
The Secretary-General of SIECA immediately called a meeting of
the Economic Council, which the Monetary Council joined.[9] The
ministers expressed alarm at the unilateral measures and accused
Costa Rica of interfering with free trade. The Manager of the
Costa Rican Central Bank explained the gravity of his government's
fiscal and balance-of-payments situations that had led to the imposition of the exchange system which, he claimed, would not affect the CACM.

---

[9]For resolutions and discussions which took place at this meeting, see SIECA, _Carta Informativa_, No. 63, pp. 5-9.

The other ministers disagreed. They held that even when member countries were forced to impose exchange restrictions, the measures should not affect regional trade, that Costa Rica's differential exchange system did so, and that the regime therefore must exempt regional trade. That is, they demanded that the old rates of exchange be used in the operations handled by the Central American Clearing House. It is reported that the ministers ordered Costa Rica to alter its measures within 48 hours or leave the Common Market. They agreed to meet again in two weeks in case Costa Rica refused to comply with the ultimatum. However, at the same time that the ministers gave their ultimatum, they agreed that Costa Rica's fiscal and balance-of-payments problems merited regional concern. The Monetary Council promised to help Costa Rica obtain regional and international financial assistance, and the ministers recommended that each of the councils study possible coordinated measures which the five countries might take to defend their balance of payments.[10]

In response, the Costa Rican Minister of Economy stated that it had not been his government's intention to interfere with free trade. He accepted the Economic Council's resolutions ad referendum, and a few days later the Costa Rican government announced its compliance. Costa Rica again handled regional trade at the old exchange rates.

The original decree's nonexemption of regional trade does not appear to have been the result of a Central Bank or governmental oversight. Bank officials drafted both the temporary and long-range measures in secret, without consulting SIECA and with the expectation of a strong reaction from the other Common Market members. One high bank official has indicated that the government intended to create a crisis in order to emphasize the seriousness of its monetary situation, to strengthen its bargaining position, and to help establish some "rules of the game" for dealing with similar cases at the regional level in the future. According to the same official, "We knew the game was lost beforehand."

---

[10] During the meeting, the Secretary-General of SIECA stated his opposition to the imposition of foreign exchange surcharges-- the proposal before the Costa Rican Assembly. Although the Costa Rican government later withdrew this proposal, it did not do so as a result of the objections of the Secretary-General, but because the opposition-controlled Assembly had modified it extensively.

IV. NATIONAL BALANCE-OF-PAYMENTS DIFFICULTIES,
FISCAL SHORTAGES, UNEQUAL BENEFITS: NICARAGUA

During 1966 and 1967, all the countries in the Central
American region suffered from deficits in their overall current
accounts.[1] As a result of a decline in cotton and coffee prices,
the deficits of Nicaragua and El Salvador grew alarmingly in
1966. El Salvador's deficit diminished in 1967, but Nicaragua's
continued to increase. The value of Guatemala's exports dropped
by 12 percent in 1967 while its imports rose by only 9 percent.
Costa Rica's deficits remained high in 1966 and 1967, although
lower than in 1965. Honduras' deficit increased, but it was low
in comparison to those of the other member countries. Net capital
inflows were sufficient to cover current account deficits in only
Costa Rica and Honduras. The other countries had to draw heavily
on their international reserves. Most important, almost 40 percent of Nicaragua's overall deficit in 1967 consisted of imbalances with its Common Market partners, as did an even larger percentage of Honduras' smaller deficit. Finally, mobilizing sufficient revenue to carry out adequate investment programs was a
problem in all the countries, except perhaps Honduras.

Faced with this general worsening of the region's economic
position, and fearful that other members might unilaterally enact
policies similar to that adopted by Costa Rica in January, the
Economic Council in August 1967 called a joint meeting with the
Ministers of Finance and Central Bank presidents for that November
Discussions at this First Tripartite Meeting were to center on
the proposals by SIECA and the Monetary Council, under study since
January, to improve Central America's fiscal and balance-of-payments situations.

By the time of the November meeting there were no signs
of improvement in the economic positions of the five CACM members.
In this context, they appear to have agreed on the need for some
regional action to support their balance of payments other than
the traditional monetary and credit measures, which had proved
to be ineffective. President Somoza of Nicaragua probably sum-
marized the opinions of the five delegations when, in his welcom-
ing address, he stated that the cost to governments of the policy

---

[1] See ECLA, The Latin American Economy in 1967 (E/CN.12/806),
especially pp. 5 and 23-26, and Cable for a detailed analysis of
the region's economic situation.

of import substitution had been great fiscal sacrifices, that the time had come to revise the policy of granting tariff exemptions to industrial firms importing raw materials, and that balance-of-payments problems had to be faced squarely.[2]

The recommendations arising out of the joint meeting were prepared by SIECA and the Monetary Council, and had been previously discussed with national economic officials. The delegates were especially concerned over the possibility of future actions similar to that announced by Costa Rica earlier in the year. Therefore they agreed with the Secretary-General of SIECA and the Executive Secretary of the Monetary Council on the need for institutionalizing a system of consultation on exchange problems, and for establishing mechanisms which would define beforehand those measures a state might take unilaterally, those requiring prior consultation, and those which could be adopted only through joint action. They assigned the Monetary Council the task of formulating bylaws to Article X of the General Treaty to this effect.[3] To facilitate the implementation of these measures, the Executive Secretary of the council recommended the creation of a Central American Reserve Fund to be built from contributions from the region and from abroad to help countries with temporary exchange

---

[2]For notes on the meeting, see SIECA, Carta Informativa, No. 74, pp. 10-19.

[3]Article X of the General Treaty reads as follows:

The Central Banks of the signatory states shall cooperate closely to prevent any currency speculation that might affect the rates of exchange and to maintain convertibility of currencies of the respective countries on a basis which, under normal conditions, shall guarantee freedom, uniformity and stability of exchange.

Should any of the signatory states establish quantitative restrictions on international monetary transfers, it shall adopt such measures as necessary to insure that such restrictions do not discriminate against the other states.

In the event of serious balance of payments difficulties which affect or are apt to affect monetary relations of payments among the signatory states, the Executive Council, at its own initiative or at the request of one of the parties, shall immediately study the problem in collaboration with the Central Banks in order to recommend to the signatory governments a satisfactory solution compatible with the maintenance of the multilateral free trade system.

difficulties. The delegates recommended that the Monetary Council study this proposal further.

Both the document prepared by SIECA and the Monetary Council on tax policy and delegate discussions pointed up the inadequacy of Central Bank credit and monetary measures in relieving pressures on foreign exchange. In light of this, the delegates agreed with the SIECA proposal that in order to cut imports unrelated to development and raise additional revenues necessary for public investment, states facing balance-of-payments and fiscal difficulties adopt a general sales tax on luxury items--the list of taxable items to be uniform throughout the region, and the rates and systems of collection consistent with free trade.

The tax proposal was neither new nor very controversial. The IDB/OAS study had suggested such taxes as a means to raise revenue, and consumption taxes on luxury items already were in effect in Costa Rica and Honduras. Moreover, under the SIECA proposal, imposition and administration of the new taxes were to remain in national hands. The SIECA proposal would serve the interests of the member states as well as those of SIECA. If several countries applied the tax, its implementation in countries where there was domestic opposition to it would be made easier--an aura of regional legitimacy would accrue to the measure. For SIECA, implementation of the tax would help it put a halt to the growing differences that had developed among the national tax structures as various countries began to apply different consumption taxes. In this way, the measure would serve as a step towards tax harmonization.

The delegates also considered a proposal from Costa Rica regarding fiscal incentives, as well as those from SIECA and the Monetary Council. Costa Rica's proposal was similar to the one it had offered to the Economic Council in September 1966. It called for a completely revised system of fiscal incentives. The revisions would include (1) the classification of industries according to regional criteria immediately rather than after seven years, (2) the elimination of tariff exemptions on the import of raw materials and intermediate goods, (3) the reduction of duties on these items to enable affected industries to operate under reasonable conditions, (4) an adequate level of protection for final products, and (5) the introduction of such practices as accelerated depreciation. Costa Rica claimed its proposal not only would help member countries overcome their balance-of-payments difficulties, but also would help to resolve fiscal shortages, stimulate industrial production (especially the production of raw materials), and eliminate problems of unfair competition. The proposal, which reopened the issue of balanced development, was not popular. However, the delegates were concerned about the increasing imports stimulated by tariff exemptions, which were undermining their countries' balance-of-payments and fiscal situations. Therefore, at the same time that they urged countries to deposit the Common Fiscal Incentives Agreement and its Preferential Treatment Protocol, they asked SIECA to study the agreement and propose reforms in it. They requested that a special analysis be made of the provisions in the agreement relating to tax and tariff exemptions.

Finally, in addition to discussing exchange, tax, and fiscal incentives measures, the delegates recommended several actions to promote exports, discussed the possibility of a more flexible tariff mechanism, and assigned a working group to make a study of SIECA's suggestion of a protocol to establish a permanent and automatic mechanism for the funding of regional institutions. The three groups of decisionmakers then agreed to meet again in six months to analyze the evolution of the fiscal and balance-of-payments situations and the extent to which their resolutions had been implemented.

During the next few months, the export-import ratios continued to deteriorate. Final 1967 figures indicated that Central America's exports as a whole had risen by only 1.1 percent at the same time that its imports had grown by 10.2 percent. The 1967 regional trade deficit amounted to U.S.$284 million--$76 million more than in 1966.[4] The fiscal situation also had grown worse. Government revenues had risen by less than 1 percent, while current costs had increased by 13.5 percent. As a result of the fiscal shortages, public investment in the region had fallen by 10 percent.

As these trends continued, a consensus appears to have developed among the national leaders on the need for more adequate policies to deal with their economic problems.[5] In order to analyze more closely their balance of payments and its implications for economic integration, the Ministers of Economy and the presidents of the Central Banks held a second joint meeting in March 1968. At this meeting they decided that immediate action at the regional level was necessary, and outlined two measures

---

[4]Figures in this paragraph are from SIECA, Carta Informativa, No. 80, p. 4. ECLA, The Latin American Economy in 1967, and Consejo Monetario Centroamericano, Boletín Estadístico, Vol. 5 (1968), report slightly different figures which, however, indicate the same trend.

[5]For example, the Presidents of Nicaragua, Costa Rica, and Honduras insisted upon the need for better policies to correct their balance-of-payments deficits in their 1968 reports to their respective national legislatures (SIECA, Carta Informativa, No. 80, pp. 3-4).

to improve their balance of payments.[6] As the major action, they
agreed unanimously to impose a so-called economic stabilization
tax--a new tax on imports from third countries--which, directly
by curbing imports and indirectly by its other fiscal and economic
repercussions, would help strengthen the balance-of-payments position of each of the five countries. The second measure was an
optional consumption tax on luxury items, which had been agreed
to previously at the First Tripartite Meeting in November. Finally, SIECA was asked to carry out some "technical tasks" concerning the measures, and then to submit the proposals as a protocol to the Second Tripartite Meeting to be held in the near
future.

SIECA prepared a Protocol on Emergency Measures to Defend
the Balance of Payments along the lines specified at the joint
meeting, then submitted it for approval. It was presented first
to the Executive Council in mid-May for final clearance by the
five governments, then two weeks later to the Second Tripartite
Meeting of the Economic Council, Monetary Council, and the Ministers of Finance.[7] Delegates to the First Tripartite Meeting had
decided to hold a second meeting to analyze the evolution of the
fiscal and balance-of-payments situations; in fact, the second
meeting was used merely to approve the final draft of measures
worked out chiefly by the Ministers of Economy with some collaboration of the Monetary Council and the technical assistance of
SIECA. On June 1, delegates to the Second Tripartite Meeting
recommended that their five governments approve the Emergency
Measures. On the same day, the Economic Council approved the
protocol, and the Executive Council resolved that as soon as
governments deposited the measure, they could impose the consumption tax without having to obtain additional authorization.[8]

Observers at the June meeting reported that the delegates
believed that if they did not approve the measures, the Common
Market would disintegrate, presumably as a result of unilateral
measures which some member states would have imposed in order to
alleviate their balance-of-payments and fiscal difficulties.[9]
Nicaragua especially had threatened to initiate measures which
would have interfered with free trade.[10]

---

[6]SIECA, Carta Informativa, No. 78, pp. 19-21; No. 79, p. 13;
and esp. No. 80, p. 3.

[7]SIECA, Carta Informativa, No. 80, pp. 3-8.

[8]Ibid., p. 8.

[9]Reporte Económico, 7 June 1968, p. 20; 14 June 1968, p. 4.

[10]The Nicaraguan economy, as indicated above, had contracted

The economic stabilization tax was a general tax of 30 percent to be imposed on all imports from third countries. It was merely an overall tariff increase to be applied both to items previously subject to tariffs and to those previously exempted under national industrial development laws or under the Central American Common Fiscal Incentives Agreement.[11]

The Emergency Measures involved no political costs. National executives would have the power to grant exemptions from the stabilization tax to firms in industries of particular importance to the economic development of the region and, with the approval of the Executive Council, firms whose operations would be gravely affected by its application. National customs houses would be in charge of its administration. To encourage deposit of the protocol, it was agreed that the first four countries to deposit it would be permitted to grant exemptions from the stabilization tax to firms enjoying exemptions under national industrial development laws or the Common Fiscal Incentives Agreement. These exemptions would lapse upon the fifth deposit. A second emergency measure allowed countries the option of imposing

---

in the mid-1960's as a consequence of the deterioration in its overall terms of trade, as well as a serious drought in 1966-67. A volcanic eruption in 1968 further reduced production of its chief export products--cotton, coffee, and sugar (Christian Science Monitor, 5 December 1968, p. 2). Although its export earnings dropped, imports of manufactured goods from third countries continued to rise. In addition, Nicaragua's trade imbalance within the Central American Common Market was larger than that of any other member state. A rise in its imports from other CACM members, stimulated by the regional policy of import substitution, had unfavorable fiscal effects. Products once imported from outside Central America were now entering Nicaragua from member states duty-free. Revenues from tariffs dropped, which contributed to a large fiscal deficit in 1967-68 (The Economist para América Latina, Vol. 2, No. 22 [October 1968], p. 37). The absence of a fully integrated market for agricultural products severely restricted the country's ability to reduce its trade imbalance within the region.

A new government took power in Nicaragua in May 1967, headed by General Anastasio Somoza. Almost immediately, Somoza responded to the depressed economic conditions by launching an austerity program intended to reduce imports of luxury items and increase fiscal revenues. It was in this context that Nicaragua pressed the other member states to adopt a protocol which would increase the Central American tariff and include some consumption taxes.

[11]For the full text of the protocol, see SIECA, Carta Informativa, No. 81.

consumption taxes of between 10 and 20 percent on several specified luxury items.

Neither measure was very controversial. The new consumption tax measure neither added to nor subtracted from the authority of regional institutions. It provided for a tax which countries might or might not impose by themselves. In agreeing to
the sales tax, the CACM member countries sidestepped the real--
and domestically explosive--issue behind fiscal losses, i.e., the
issue of fundamental tax reform. The economic stabilization tax
raised tariffs to curb imports, and thereby prevent a worsening
balance-of-payments situation. Both measures were traditional
responses to fiscal and payments difficulties. They involved
neither changes in the traditional economic structures in the
region nor any surrender of national authority.

These measures may have been politically acceptable, but
as one keen economic analyst has noted, their economic consequences
were difficult to forecast. With respect to the fiscal and balance-of-payments problems, Cable has offered this criticism of
the Emergency Measures (San José) Protocol:

> It might help to solve the relatively minor revenue prob-
> lem, which could be solved more easily by raising income
> tax, tightening up on concessions, introducing property
> taxes, or levying export taxes on surplus commodities.
> The revenue effect of the San José import-duty surcharge
> is uncertain and will only be really effective if the
> effect on the volume of imports is small, which makes
> little sense from a balance of payments point of view;
> in increased direct taxation there is no such conflict
> of interest. The taxes on locally produced goods could
> help revenue and also reduce the protective effect of
> the increased import duty; otherwise there would be an
> additional incentive to produce, very uneconomically,
> various luxury consumer goods: on the other hand they
> could be used against products from other CACM coun-
> tries, thus hampering regional trade. The increased
> duty makes Central America an even more heavily pro-
> tected area than before, hindering future links with the
> LAFTA; it may also hinder new investment, and raise the
> cost of present plants, unless remission for imports
> necessary for industry is speedily and extensively ob-
> tained. Finally, the San José taxes may have infla-
> tionary effects if prices are given a permanent upward
> twist, though presumably it is intended that the mea-
> sures should have the opposite effect, of reducing real
> incomes and therefore expenditure. So, as a revenue
> measure the Protocol is almost certainly tending in the
> wrong direction--away from direct taxation; the improve-
> ment to the overall balance of payments resulting from

reduced expenditure is unpredictable and may be
achieved at high cost to the economies.[12]

During the formulation and negotiation of the Emergency
Measures, neither national economic officials nor SIECA consulted
with national or regional business associations. In what appears
to have been an attempt to avoid almost certain vocal opposition
to the measures before their passage, economic officials kept
business groups out of the decision-making process. Only after
the delegates to the Second Tripartite Meeting passed the Emergency Measures did they receive FECAICA officials to "discuss"
with them the urgency of the actions they had taken.[13] National
economic officials did not appoint representatives of the national
business associations to national delegations for the meetings at
which discussions of these proposals took place, although they
had been appointed to such national delegations in the past. Finally, neither national nor regional officials publicly reported
with any breadth on the proposals made at the regional level until
quite late in the decision-making process.

The business groups were slow to take action, and appear
to have operated with outdated information. Not until May, when
national economic officials already had agreed, at least informally, on the measures to be taken, did FECAICA send a letter to
the Economic Council expressing its complete disagreement with
the proposals presented at the First Tripartite Meeting of the
previous November.[14] In its communique, FECAICA opposed both
the Costa Rican proposal and the suggestion of a general sales
tax on luxury items. It claimed that eliminating tariff exemptions would threaten the infant industries and create the sorry
precedent that industrial benefits once granted could be abolished.
With regard to the proposed sales tax, it held that a chief reason
for insufficient government revenues was governmental ineffective-
ness in collecting taxes already in effect. The implementation
of these new measures, according to FECAICA, would undermine business confidence in market institutions and lead to a reduction in
investment in the region. The communique decried the fact that
no one had sought the opinion of businessmen on the issue. This
note and the discussion with delegates to the Second Tripartite
Meeting after the Emergency Measures had been decided upon con-
stitute the whole of FECAICA's participation in the decision.

---

[12]Cable, pp. 345-346.

[13]Reporte Económico (El Salvador), 7 June 1968, Comunicado de
Consejo Económico, p. 19.

[14]Reporte Económico (El Salvador), 24 May 1968, p. 9.

Nicaragua urged the members to ratify and deposit the San José Protocol quickly, but met with little success. The Nicaraguan Congress approved the protocol within 48 hours of its signature, and the government deposited it one month later. It acted with such speed that there was no time for domestic opposition to form. In any case, domestic opposition would have had little influence on government decision-making in Nicaragua-- probably less than in any of the other four member countries.

In Honduras, the business sector, centered in the North Coast, roundly opposed ratification of the protocol.[15] In any case, the Honduran government refused to deposit any important agreement until all member states had deposited the Protocol on Preferential Treatment signed in 1966. The industrial sector in Guatemala also was opposed to the San José Protocol, but it was more concerned with the issue of terrorism.[16]

In El Salvador, the merchants, industrialists, unions, and Christian Democrats opposed the imposition of new consumption taxes.[17] The Chamber of Commerce and Industry unanimously opposed the new taxes and requested that the Minister of Economy pay attention to its arguments before ratifying the protocol; the Chamber also criticized SIECA's "secrecy" in handling the entire issue.[18] The Salvadorean Industrial Association (ASI) asked the government to establish a commission to examine the protocol, and requested that the Association be represented on it.[19] Meanwhile, the Salvadorean Minister of Economy strongly urged ratification in several speeches.[20]

---

[15] New York Times, 20 January 1969, Sec. C, p. 66; The Economist para América Latina, Vol. 2, No. 23 (13 November 1968), p. 37. The Honduran government's later imposition of some of the consumption taxes included in the protocol led in October to a business- and labor-supported general strike in San Pedro Sula. The government declared a state of siege and broke the stoppage, but tension between the business and government sectors remained high throughout the year.

[16] The Economist para América Latina, 13 November 1968, p. 37.

[17] Ibid.

[18] Reporte Económico, 21 June 1968, p. 11.

[19] Reporte Económico, 2 August 1968, p. 3.

[20] The Minister of Economy supported the measure, for example, in a press conference and in a television speech reported in Reporte Económico, 7 June 1968, p. 4, and 28 June 1968, p. 3.

Although the Costa Rican President favored the measures, and the government had imposed sales taxes similar to those in the protocol one year before, the Partido de Liberación Nacional (PLN)--the political opposition in control of the National Assembly--charged that the measures were a tax on the poor, and therefore opposed the protocol.[21] Even refusal by the U.S. and other lending agencies to release large-scale loans until Costa Rica ratified the 30 percent surcharge, and thus stabilized its fiscal and monetary situation, had little effect on the National Assembly.[22] At the regional level, FECAICA officials set up a working group to examine the agreement.[23]

In sum, one month after subscription by the Ministers of Economy, only Nicaragua had deposited the protocol. The chances for its rapid implementation throughout the region were virtually nil.

Pressed by severe balance-of-payments and fiscal difficulties, irked by the delay in the ratification and deposit of the Emergency Measures, and accusing El Salvador, Guatemala, and Honduras of exporting items not of regional origin duty-free to Nicaragua, the Somoza government unilaterally imposed several measures which affected regional free trade. On June 21 it decreed consumption taxes of 10 and 20 percent on the same items as those in the San José Protocol, and levied a consumption tax of up to 30 percent on a specified list of articles nationally and regionally produced, as well as imported from outside the area.[24] In effect, it unilaterally adopted the new protocol. It also imposed a 5 percent sales tax on all articles of Central American origin entering Nicaragua except those already covered by the 10 and 20 percent tax and other specified items. The sales tax applied to similar articles produced in Nicaragua or imported from third countries. Almost immediately, Nicaraguan border officials delayed or turned back trucks filled with regionally produced items, demanding payment of the new duties.

Differential bases and forms of collection stipulated in the decrees appeared to favor Nicaraguan-produced articles. The several taxes, when applied ad valorem, were calculated on the CIF value of imports; they were computed on the basis of the

---

[21] The Economist para América Latína, 13 November 1968, p. 37.

[22] Ibid.; New York Times, 20 January 1969, Sec. C., p. 66.

[23] Reporte Económico, 14 June 1968, p. 1.

[24] Reporte Económico, 28 June 1968, pp. 1 and 16; La Gaceta, Diario Oficial de Nicaragua, 21 June 1968.

factory price for nationally produced items. Taxes on imported items were to be paid at the customs house; those on national production were to be collected at the national revenue office.

The other member states reacted to the Nicaraguan measures quickly, with disfavor but also with restraint. In the presence of the Nicaraguan delegate, but outside the agenda of the July meeting of the Executive Council, delegates from the other four states expressed their concern that the use of different bases and forms of collection might make the taxes discriminatory.[25] Some of the delegates charged that Nicaragua was unilaterally imposing consumption taxes on some items produced in the region but not in Nicaragua itself. They suggested that this was perhaps a violation of Article VI of the General Treaty. In addition, they questioned whether Nicaragua was applying consumption taxes to nationally as well as to regionally produced items. Finally, they questioned Nicaragua's right to unilaterally put into effect the San José Protocol.

Only a few weeks later, Nicaragua agreed to withdraw the most controversial of its taxes. El Salvador had sent an official mission to Managua which, it appeared, had reestablished trade between the two countries for the item--rice--which had been most affected by the Nicaraguan decree. Days later, the Central American Presidents held a special meeting to discuss the region's financial problems and the faltering integration effort. In the statement issued after their meeting, they pledged to press for rapid passage and deposit of the San José Protocol and other regional agreements which were pending. President Johnson had attended the meeting and had promised additional loans for the region as a whole and for each of the member countries. At this point, it appears that Nicaragua withdrew at least those taxes which fell most heavily on agricultural products imported from the other member states.[26]

Nevertheless, during the months following the Central American Presidents' Meeting, interruptions in trade between Nicaragua and its neighbors not only continued, but spread to other items.[27] Nicaragua continued, as it had since June, to

---

[25] The complaints of each of the four representatives are reported in *Reporte Económico*, 2 August 1968, p. 5.

[26] *Latin American Newsletter* (London), 12 July 1968, p. 223. *Comercio Exterior*, Vol. 19, No. 3 (March 1969), p. 203, refers to the meeting of the Presidents as a "salvage operation" (operación de salvamiento).

[27] The interruptions in trade are discussed in SIECA, *Carta*

block rice imports from Guatemala, even though a SIECA investigation had indicated that Guatemala had not imported rice from outside the region and a majority in the Executive Council had voted to reestablish free trade for the item. Nicaragua also suspended the free trade of clothing made in Honduras with synthetic fibers, charging that Honduras had exempted a disproportionate amount of the raw materials from tariffs. A majority in the Executive Council voted to reestablish free trade, but the Nicaraguan delegate claimed that additional investigations were necessary. The Nicaraguan government blocked the entry of shirts imported from a Honduran firm, claiming that the country was exporting them at undervalued prices. It requested of the Executive Council that it be allowed to place a bond in an amount equivalent to the common tariff on the article; the council rejected the Nicaraguan request. In retaliation for these actions taken by Nicaragua, the Honduran government closed its borders to biscuits manufactured in that country. Finally, Nicaragua put a halt to its imports of Costa Rican maize and beans, charging that Costa Rica had imported some of these products from Mexico.

Nicaragua was not the only member to create obstacles to free trade. In late 1968, El Salvador closed its borders to Guatemalan cigarettes. Costa Rica, accusing El Salvador of exporting rice imported from outside the region, cut off rice imports from that country and later from all Central America. In retaliation, El Salvador blocked imports of Costa Rican dairy products. Costa Rica also suspended its imports of Guatemalan cigarettes and cut off trade of several Honduran-produced items in reprisal for that country's suspension of trade of several articles made in Costa Rica.

On the one hand, the increase in conflicts was probably due to the reaction of the Nicaraguan government to the refusal or slowness of the other member states to deposit the San José Protocol. Irrespective of the pledges of the Central American Presidents and the promise of additional U.S. loans, by mid-October no other state had deposited the agreement. Consequently, the Somoza government acted unilaterally in a way to alleviate the country's deteriorating trade balance and fiscal shortages; other member states took retaliatory measures. On the other hand, although they had not yet deposited the protocol, Honduras imposed a 10 percent consumption tax on items covered by the agreement, and Guatemala established new taxes on national and imported articles.[28]

Informativa, No. 82, pp. 2-7, and No. 84, pp. 9-11; *Latin American Newsletter*, 27 December 1968, p. 409; and *Reporte Economico*, 15 November 1968, 22 November 1968, and 13 December 1968.

[28] SIECA, *Carta Informativa*, No. 83, pp. 16-17.

Exporter countries in the region charged discrimination over forms of collection for the new taxes, and retaliated by blocking free trade of one or another product.

In an attempt to resolve what was becoming a crisis situation, the Secretary-General of SIECA, accompanied by the Salvadorean Minister of Economy, traveled to Guatemala, Honduras, and Costa Rica in October. Their objectives were to determine possibilities for the early ratification and deposit of the protocol, to observe local reaction to the imposition of the new consumption taxes, and to try to convoke an Economic Council meeting in order to find some way to coordinate the new consumption taxes at the regional level and to write a bylaw covering the form of collection.[29]

They found the possibilities for early implementation of the San José Protocol dim. El Salvador and Guatemala deposited the agreement at the end of October; Guatemala deposited the Protocol on Preferential Treatment for Honduras as well. Although Honduras had already ratified the San José Protocol, it refused to deposit both it and the Common Fiscal Incentives Agreement until El Salvador deposited the Preferential Treatment Protocol. Meanwhile, the opposition-dominated Costa Rican National Assembly still refused to ratify the San José agreement. Reacting to this deadlock, the Somoza government beginning in late 1968 refused to attend CACM meetings until the other member states deposited several agreements which were outstanding, especially the San José Protocol.

Two presidential meetings in Central America and a statement by President Somoza in December deepened the sense of crisis throughout the region. After a joint meeting, the Presidents of Nicaragua and Costa Rica issued a communique in which they decried the institutional and operational "incompletion" of the CACM as unfavorable to their countries, and warned that in the absence of the market's completion they might be forced to adopt measures "in defense of the interests of the people of Costa Rica and Nicaragua."[30] The Presidents threatened to press for a restructuring of the Common Market's institutional framework if the market were not soon perfected. To complete the CACM, they urged that still outstanding protocols be deposited, that deposit of integration agreements not be utilized as a bargaining instrument for the negotiation of later agreements, that the Common Fiscal Incentives Agreement be modified after its deposit, that the Protocol on Basic Cereals be revised, that a permanent court soon

[29] SIECA, Carta Informativa, No. 85, pp. 14-15.

[30] SIECA, Carta Informativa, No. 87, pp. 1-2.

be established to deal with the day-to-day problems of integration, and that importance be attached to the agricultural sector
in the integration instruments.

A few weeks later, Somoza, in a television speech, charged
that one cause of Nicaragua's economic problems was the CACM and
the bad faith of the other members.[31] He called for a complete
review of the structure of the Common Market, and insisted upon
the need to limit free trade between Nicaragua on the one hand and
El Salvador and Guatemala on the other. Shortly thereafter, the
General journeyed to Honduras for another presidential meeting.
In their joint communique the two chief executives largely reiterated the demands arising out of the other, earlier meeting:
they stressed the need for the deposit of pending regional agreements, reform of Common Market organs, and greater regional empha-
sis on the agricultural sector.[32] The two Presidents urged that
the five member countries agree to hold meetings at which measures
would be effected which would structurally and operationally complete the CACM, with priority being given to the revision of the
Basic Cereals Protocol and to action facilitating more foreign
and national investment. The second communique was less threatening and more hopeful in tone than the first.

At the end of January 1969, the Secretary-General of SIECA
expressed his concern at the growing crisis.[33] To preserve and expand the level of regional trade, he urged the five member states
to launch a program in which they would coordinate their guaran-
teed prices of basic cereals, deposit and reform the Common Fiscal
Incentives Agreement, harmonize sales and consumption taxes already in effect, and remove obstacles to free trade, such as certain forms of tax collection which were acting as customs barriers.

The establishment of an integration court--suggested by
Somoza and included in the communique issued by him and President
Trejos of Costa Rica--was not popular with all the member coun-
tries. At the Fourth Meeting of the Central American Foreign
Ministers in early February 1969, held chiefly to elect a new
Secretary-General for ODECA, Nicaragua formally proposed the im-
mediate formation of a court to serve as the final recourse in
integration disputes.[34] The Honduran minister claimed that he

---

[31]Latin American Newsletter, 27 December 1968, p. 409.

[32]SIECA, Carta Informativa, No. 87, pp. 2-5.

[33]SIECA, Carta Informativa, No. 88, p. 1.

[34]For additional information on events surrounding the proposal,
see Latin American Newsletter, 28 February 1969, p. 65, and SIECA,
Carta Informativa, No. 89, pp. 1-2.

could not support the court's immediate establishment, but would need additional time to consult with his government. His viewpoint--that additional consultation time was required--prevailed. The meeting adjourned abruptly without any favorable action being taken. A short time later, four of the five Ministers of Economy (the Nicaraguan minister did not attend) met informally in a secret session to discuss the proposed court, but apparently concluded only that the issue required further consultations. Since no headway had been made, the meeting of the Foreign Ministers called to consider the issue in late February adjourned immediately.

By late February, then, consideration of the proposed court was delayed indefinitely. At the same time, free trade of several items between Nicaragua and the other CACM countries remained suspended. In addition, the Costa Rican National Assembly had rejected the San José Protocol twice by a large majority. According to the provisions of the Costa Rican constitution, the National Assembly could consider the protocol only one more time; then it would become a dead issue.[35] Honduras still refused to deposit the San José agreement until El Salvador deposited the Preferential Treatment Protocol.[36] And although they had deposited the San José Protocol, El Salvador and Guatemala, utilizing the protocol's transitory article, had suspended application of the 30 percent tax on imports until deposit by the others.[37] Only Nicaragua was applying the tax.

In this context, and after the Costa Rican Assembly had rejected the San José Protocol for the second time, the Nicaraguan government claimed that it was operating in a disadvantageous position vis-à-vis the other member states. It threatened to take some still undefined action to protect itself. Somoza at a public meeting denounced those countries refusing or delaying ratification as "bad friends" and declared that "we have acted loyally and sincerely sought integration, but we are not ready to sacrifice ourselves to the point of taking off our shirt for others to don."[38] At about the same time, another member of the Somoza family wrote in a Managua newspaper that Nicaragua had

---

[35]Latin American Newsletter, 28 February 1969, p. 66.

[36]The Honduran Minister of Economy explicitly stated that this was the position of his government (SIECA, Carta Informativa, No. 89, p. 6).

[37]Latin American Newsletter, 21 February 1969, p. 59.

[38]Latin American Newsletter, 28 February 1969, p. 66.

lost U.S.$48 million in 1968 to the "unscrupulous industrialists of El Salvador and Guatemala."[39]

Finally, President Somoza, citing the need to defend Nicaragua's balance of payments and improve its fiscal situation, on February 26 decreed a "compensatory consumption tax" applicable to most items originating in the rest of Central America for an amount equivalent to the tariffs in effect in Nicaragua on July 1, 1955.[40] This decree reestablished a tariff barrier in the region. As justification for the measure, the government in the preamble to the decree indicated that revenue losses due to regional import substitution were seriously affecting the country's development program. It charged that the Common Market had not led, as it should have, to the establishment of a customs union which equitably distributed its import revenues so as to promote the balanced development of regional trade and provide sufficient revenues for each country to carry out its development program. Instead, as a result of the incompletion of the CACM, privileged sectors had been created which were making large profits to the detriment of the other sectors and the development of other member countries.

Although the other four member states initially responded to the Nicaraguan decree in a conciliatory manner, the Nicaraguan government refused to reverse its action. At the meeting of the five Ministers of Economy scheduled previously for early March to resolve the then growing crisis in the CACM, the delegates focused all their attention on the new decree.[41] The four ministers, noting the unfavorable consequences of the Nicaraguan action, urged Nicaragua to withdraw or to suspend its measure, with the promise that the four other countries would deposit the outstanding agreements. To emphasize their pledges, the Salvadorean minister announced that his country would deposit the Preferential Treatment Protocol within two weeks; the Honduran minister reiterated that his government would deposit the Common Fiscal Incentives Agreement and its Protocol, the San José Protocol, and the

---

[39] Latin American Newsletter, 14 March 1969, p. 85.

[40] SIECA, Carta Informativa, No. 89, p. 1. The decree stipulated that the new tax was to be calculated on the CIF value of an item and was to be paid at the point of entry into Nicaragua. It excepted from the tax a list of agricultural and other essential items as well as goods manufactured by industries covered by the Agreement on Integration Industries.

[41] SIECA, Carta Informativa, No. 89, pp. 1-7, includes a report on the meeting and reproduces the official declarations of the Nicaraguan Minister of Economy and that of the four other ministers.

rest of the pending agreements immediately after El Salvador honored its pledge; the Costa Rican minister promised to make a greater effort to solve the problem of the San José Protocol in his country; and the Guatemalan minister noted that his government had only a few agreements outstanding.

But the Nicaraguan minister claimed that due to the fiscal situation which was threatening his country, the new decree was "indispensable in order to compensate, at least in part, for the fiscal losses due to its participation in the Common Market."[4] In discussions and in the communique he issued at the end of the meeting, the Nicaraguan minister demanded the following: (1) rapid deposit of pending agreements; (2) immediate revision of instruments such as the Common Fiscal Incentives Agreement and the Basic Cereals Protocol; (3) examination of the possibility of enacting compensatory taxes at the regional level on articles enjoying free regional trade in order to allow states to recover part of the fiscal income lost as a result of integration while maintaining a preferential margin for Central American items as compared with those from third countries; and (4) establishment of the unanimity rule in Common Market organs in voting on any measure which might have fiscal repercussions. Finally, the minister suggested that the Economic and Executive Councils remain in permanent session to deal with any problem which might arise during the crisis.

In response to Nicaragua's intransigence, the four ministers, acting in accord with Articles XI and XIII of the General Treaty, suspended free trade between Nicaragua and the other member countries by imposing a bond in the amount of the common tariff on goods originating in that country. In the case of non-equalized items, the bond was equivalent to the national tariffs in effect. The four ministers expressed their surprise at the timing of the Nicaraguan measures: the March meeting of the Economic Council had already been scheduled and was to have studied ways to resolve various problems in the market when Nicaragua published its decree. Although the action they took was strong, the overall tone of their communique was conciliatory. They expressed their "sorrow" at being forced to authorize the bonds; they were pleased that Nicaragua was willing to discuss ways to resolve the crisis at regional meetings, signifying an end to its boycott of CACM organs; they agreed to maintain the Economic Council in permanent session to help reestablish normality in the region; and they announced their intention to remove the bonds as soon as Nicaragua withdrew the compensatory tax.[43] Nevertheless, as a

---

[42]Ibid., p. 2

[43]In light of the two preceding sections of this paper, the second point of the communique of the four ministers is amusing,

result of the Nicaraguan decree and the counter-measures taken by the four ministers, trade between Nicaragua and the others dwindled.[44]

During the next few weeks contact among the four other members, Nicaragua, and SIECA functionaries was continuous and informal, often by telephone.[45] Moreover, the Salvadorean government acted as if an understanding existed between the four and Nicaragua according to which the deposit of agreements would be followed by withdrawal of the Nicaraguan decree. Although the Nicaraguan government denied the existence of any such understanding,[46] on March 14 El Salvador, acting on the assumption of its existence, deposited four agreements, including the Protocol on Preferential Treatment for Honduras. On the same day Honduras deposited the Common Fiscal Incentives Agreement, the Preferential Treatment Protocol, and the San José Protocol.

Finally, one week later and after three days of debate at an Emergency Meeting of the Economic Council, the five Ministers

---

although Nicaragua no doubt found it hypocritical:

> We stress that the treaties and agreements of economic integration deserve the most profound respect from our governments. In this sense, we point out that we have always tried to resolve the problems which we confront in the Common Market within the established legal framework. This relates, for example, to the solutions we have sought and continue trying to find to the serious fiscal problems which our economies face; to the way in which the problem of balanced development was dealt with by Honduras, and in which measures tending to alleviate that problem were adopted; and to the experience that we had only two years ago in the case of the exchange measures adopted by Costa Rica, the application of which to Central American transactions had to be revoked by that country so that the economic unity of the Common Market would be maintained (SIECA, Carta Informativa, No. 89, pp. 4-5).

[44] Costa Rica, for example, exported $70,432 in clothing to Nicaragua in February; after Nicaragua imposed the new tariffs in March, the amount fell to $31,755 (Latin American Newsletter, 27 June 1969, p. 207).

[45] Reporte Económico, 14 March 1969, p. 1.

[46] Reporte Económico, 28 March 1969, p. 4.

of Economy reached an agreement which reestablished free trade.[47] On the one hand, the Nicaraguan minister announced that his government would reform its tax in a way which would make it compatible with General Treaty provisions yet would ensure itself an equivalent revenue, considered crucial in light of its fiscal deficit. To satisfy both criteria, it proposed to change its measure into a consumption tax applicable not only to products of Central American origin but also to similar items manufactured in Nicaragua and to those imported from third countries. It promised that in cases in which the taxable item was produced in any of the other member countries but not in Nicaragua it would impose the tax only after authorization from the Executive Council. Lastly, it indicated that it would study the possibility of exempting goods already subject to consumption taxes, broadening the general list of exempted items, unifying in one instrument the different consumption taxes in effect in Nicaragua, and reducing or eliminating the tax in instances in which it was demonstrated that its application seriously affected free trade or production in the rest of the region. In response to the reform promised by Nicaragua, the other ministers withdrew the sanctions imposed the previous month.

In addition to the promised Nicaraguan reform and the lifting of sanctions, the five ministers pledged to push the CACM to a new stage of development, among other reasons, "in order to resolve existing problems" and "to prevent the repetition of critical situations which affect the stability of the Common Market and which recently have been occurring every time with greater frequency." As objectives for this next stage, they set the gradual establishment of a customs union, coordination of their national industrial, agricultural, monetary, and infrastructure policies, creation of a common capital stock market, development of conditions promoting mobility of labor, and joint defense of their exports.

The ministers agreed to an Immediate Action Plan which outlined the first phase of the work required. The Plan included as immediate goals several demands made earlier by Nicaragua-- for example, the need to incorporate in the CACM additional elements promoting balanced development, to reform the Common Fiscal Incentives Agreement, and to promote a more balanced integration between agricultural and industrial development, in part by making more effective application of the Basic Cereals Protocol. The ministers assigned SIECA the important tasks of carrying out the

---

[47]SIECA, Carta Informativa, No. 90, pp. 2-4, includes the Nicaraguan statement, that of the other four ministers which outlined the terms of the agreement, and the text of the "Immediate Action Plan of the Program of Central American Economic Integration."

necessary studies, making suggestions, and developing a working schedule for the Plan.[48] Finally, to help avoid conflicts like that which had occurred, the ministers agreed to formulate a bylaw to Article VI of the General Treaty which would include general norms for the application and administration of domestic consumption taxes in the five countries.

Thus the crisis appeared to be resolved in a manner which resulted in greater consolidation of the CACM, satisfied some of the demands of the less developed members, and involved a potential expansion of the scope of integration. As a result of pressure from Nicaragua, member countries deposited several important integration agreements. Both the Common Fiscal Incentives Agreement and its Protocol on Preferential Treatment for Honduras finally became legally effective--the former seven years and the latter three years after it had been signed. Honduras, which on its own had been unable to obtain Salvadorean deposit of the protocol, finally succeeded as a result of Nicaraguan intransigence. Although Nicaragua was unsuccessful in pressuring Costa Rica to deposit and thereby put into effect the San José Protocol, that was only because the opposition-dominated Costa Rican National Assembly was against the measure for domestic political reasons. Further action by Nicaragua seemed unlikely to alter that situation. However, Nicaragua did succeed in forcing the others to deposit several major agreements. Furthermore, it obtained promises in the form of the Immediate Action Plan for satisfaction of several other of its demands. For El Salvador, Guatemala, and Costa Rica, resolution of the crisis meant an end to the threat of a geographically divided regional market and reestablishment of what was for them a highly profitable trade with Nicaragua. In terms of concrete actions, the cost to them of the resolution of the crisis did not appear high. On the other hand, actual achievement of even some of the objectives of the Plan would expand considerably the scope of the CACM.

The Nicaraguan private sector and those of the other members had responded to the original Nicaraguan decree with strong support for the CACM. Representatives of the private sector in Nicaragua requested--unsuccessfully--that the government delay imposition of the February decree until other member countries had additional time to deposit pending agreements.[49] After Somoza disregarded their request and imposed the measure, the Nicaraguan Chamber of Commerce, Chamber of Construction, Association of

---

[48] SIECA was to submit a proposed working schedule for the Plan to the next meeting of the Economic Council, and its study and suggestions regarding a customs union by the end of 1969.

[49] Latin American Newsletter, 28 March 1969, p. 98.

Banking Institutions, and Development Institute issued a joint
declaration in which they vigorously defended Nicaragua's continued participation in the Common Market as essential for the
country's development, and urged resolution of the problems af-
flicting integration.[50]   In addition, representatives of the
Nicaraguan private sector traveled throughout Central America on
so-called goodwill missions to speak with officials of business
organizations and governments, urging them to deposit the outstanding agreements and thereby resolve the crisis.[51]

Business associations in other member countries and in
the region as a whole also responded to the Nicaraguan decree.
For example, the Costa Rican Chamber of Commerce, not always a
defender of the CACM, condemned the Nicaraguan action.[52]   The
Salvadorean Industrial Association (ASI), probably the most active
business organization in the region, issued a statement in which
it explored the reasons behind the Nicaraguan decree.[53]   The basic
problem, it stated, was that the economic growth of the five CACM
members, instead of being complementary, had become competitive,
thereby generating forces contrary to integration which tried to
protect their own markets. As a remedy, ASI suggested that free
mobility of the factors of production, along with the more rapid
development of infrastructures, would lead to a more logical and
complementary localization of industry. It would appear, at least
to the outside observer, that this so-called remedy would result
primarily in greater benefits to more industrialized El Salvador.
The Central American Chamber of Industry (FECAICA) also expressed
anxiety over the sudden and unilateral Nicaraguan action which,
it said, could seriously affect industry in the region.[54]   But
all in all, there is no evidence that the Nicaraguan private sector or business associations in other countries influenced the
parties involved in the resolution of the crisis.

When, a few days after the Economic Council meeting, the
Nicaraguan government specified and began to apply its reformed
tax, it became clear that the base on which the new tax was
calculated, as well as its form of collection, still favored

---

[50]SIECA, Carta Informativa, No. 90, pp. 26-27.

[51]For indications that this was the reason behind the Nicaraguan
visits, see Reporte Económico, "Noticiero y Comentario," 25 April
1969, p. 10.

[52]Latin American Newsletter, 28 March 1969, p. 98.

[53]Reporte Económico, 7 March 1969, p. 12.

[54]Reporte Económico, 14 March 1969, p. 1.

local industries. Whereas Nicaraguan businessmen could pay the tax over time to the National Office of Revenue, businessmen from the other member countries had to pay it in full at the point of entry into Nicaragua.[55] In addition, the ad valorem tax was calculated on the basis of factory prices for Nicaraguan products rather than on the CIF value for imports.

Protests within Nicaragua, as well as in the region as a whole, followed application of the new tax. Inside Nicaragua, imposition of the measure led to large increases in the cost of living and to difficulties for the clothing and construction industries.[56] After several clothing manufacturers threatened to close their factories, and unemployment in the construction industry rose, the Minister of Economy announced that errors had been made in the announced list of items subject to the tax. He reduced the rates on clothing and building materials.

On the regional level, representatives of the other four member countries claimed that in its application of the tax Nicaragua was discriminating against them and favoring national products. They expressed doubt as to the compatibility of the measure with Article VI of the General Treaty. At the May Executive Council meeting, representatives from the other four countries asked SIECA to examine the unfavorable effects of the application of the tax on them.[57] ASI and the Salvadorean Chamber of Commerce, as well as other business associations, brought similar complaints to the Executive Council.[58] The Nicaraguan representative disagreed with these charges, claiming that the new decree was in accord with the laws of his country and with the juridical framework of the CACM. But the council ordered SIECA to carry out an investigation of the various domestic taxes in effect in Nicaragua and the other four countries and to report on its findings at the next council meeting so that the council could take action to ensure free trade--that is, so it could submit what it saw as necessary proposals to the Economic Council.

When tensions between Honduras and El Salvador rose in the summer of 1969, the crisis in the CACM continued unresolved. Regardless of the pledge of several months earlier, the Immediate

---

[55] Reporte Económico, 28 March 1969, p. 10.

[56] Latin American Newsletter, 25 April 1969, p. 135. This report also indicates that as a result of the new measure, exports from the other CACM countries to Nicaragua were declining.

[57] SIECA, Carta Informativa, No. 92, p. 9.

[58] Reporte Económico, 6 June 1969, p. 1.

Action Plan remained inoperative, and Nicaragua was applying a tax which violated the basic principle behind the Common Market--regional free trade, especially of manufactures.

V. CONCLUSION

Our analysis of the three CACM crises has revealed several common threads running through all of them. Taken together, these threads form a pattern or common sequence of events which characterizes the emergence, processing, and outcome of conflicts arising out of the highly controversial balanced development or unequal benefits issue.

The most striking characteristic of the Common Market evidenced in these examples of actor behavior has been the continuous and stubborn reliance by the member countries on the operation of unregulated market forces to achieve industrial growth once trade barriers have been removed and a common tariff constructed. National economic officials committed themselves in 1960 to the free trade movement of goods and services. They have been able to agree on little else, and SIECA has not been able to arrange a significant expansion of that commitment.

Reliance by national economic officials in the early 1960's on uncoordinated action by private enterprise to achieve industrialization had, as a consequence, some unplanned for-- but not wholly unexpected--economic changes. As desired by national and regional officials, intra-regional trade grew impressively. The bulk of this trade, stimulated by policies of import substitution, came to consist of manufactures rather than foodstuffs. Additional foreign investment also appeared to be attracted to the region.

But there were other consequences as well. The great bulk of the new industrial investment did not flow to the less developed members but continued to be attracted to the traditional centers of the more developed members. In addition, regional trading patterns changed. The less developed countries continued to export their agricultural products to the more developed countries in the region with almost no help from the new tariff. But, beginning in 1960, they began to import large amounts of manufactures from their slightly more developed neighbors, often at a higher cost than that previously paid for similar items imported from third countries and without receiving tariff revenues previously collected on such items. Even in the early 1960's the two least developed countries in the CACM-- Honduras and Nicaragua--began to experience deficits in their regional balance of payments. Meanwhile, national competition over granting fiscal incentives and the growth of assembly plants with little value added intensified the balance-of-payments and fiscal problems of two other members, Guatemala and Costa Rica.

In addition to these economic consequences of the operation of the Common Market, there also appear to have been some changes in national goals. Most important, economic officials in the less developed countries appear to have adopted the ECLA- and SIECA-stressed objective of rapid industrial development as their primary national objective. At the same time, officials in the relatively more developed member states intensified their commitment to the same goal. Consequently, in both sets of countries officials became increasingly sensitive to economic changes which might affect their development. All actors judged the operation of the CACM according to the extent to which it aided or hindered their development relative to the other members. In the three crises discussed in this study, national economic and/ or political officials perceived unfavorable aspects of their economic situations--regional trade imbalances, overall balance-of-payments deficits, fiscal shortages--as a consequence of or exacerbated by the structure of the CACM.

There was no direct relationship, however, between worsening economic conditions at the national level, on the one hand, and demands and disruptive actions at the regional level, on the other. Honduras pressed for preferential treatment when it was experiencing its first regional trade imbalances, but in the context of favorable conditions for its exports, which were providing it with high growth rates. When in a somewhat similar position, Nicaragua strongly supported the CACM. Although Costa Rica was suffering from foreign exchange and fiscal shortages, as it had for several years, its exports to third countries were increasing after a few years in which they had been in decline, and its exports to the rest of Central America--mainly manufactures-- were growing rapidly when it announced its potentially disruptive measures. Nicaragua, on the other hand, was experiencing increasing imbalances in regional trade, external trade deficits, and fiscal shortages when it made its initial demands in the late 1960's.

Changed economic conditions, then, do not appear to account wholly for the sharp changes in actor strategies after 1964. The introduction of new demands and disruptive strategies was probably associated more with recent changes in government than with worsening economic conditions. New officials in new governments who had not been participants in the negotiations of the original integration agreements and in the numerous subsequent regional meetings made the demands around which each of the conflicts centered. Officials in new governments were more likely to perceive integration as exacerbating their economic problems and to use disruptive tactics than were their predecessors. The new governments in Honduras, Costa Rica, and Nicaragua clearly demonstrated that they did not view free trade as a "sacred cow," as had previous governments. In these instances, changes of government interfered with integrative learning.

Member countries responded in different ways and Common Market organs utilized different methods in dealing with "Common Market problems" than with problems other than those involving direct obstacles to free trade. On the one hand, member countries demonstrated a high level of mutual responsiveness in seeking the resolution of "Common Market problems." SIECA quickly and oftentimes informally resolved the day-to-day conflicts over national origin and labeling and similar problems which interfered with free trade. In those instances in which it was unable to achieve rapid settlement, an informal procedure involving the Executive Council, a council working group, and SIECA was developed by which such problems generally were resolved. Although they had the right to do so, member countries almost never appealed decisions on "Common Market problems" to the Economic Council. As a consequence of the technical competence of its investigations of these problems, the adroit manner in which it settled them, and the political wisdom evidenced by its Secretaries-General, SIECA gained a reputation for technical skill and political trustworthiness.

But on issues of unequal benefits--issues not directly related to free trade, on which there had been no inital clear commitment for joint action and which member countries perceived as involving potential national costs--member countries, acting through the Economic Council, did not evidence a similar level of mutual responsiveness and relied chiefly on delay and avoidance as methods of conflict resolution, apparently with the hope that the evolution of market forces would resolve the issue or that the complainant country would tire and withdraw its demands. The complainant, in turn, relied on blackmail and escalation to force its partners to act.

As with tough "Common Market problems," the members referred these issues to SIECA for "study." Following a procedure similar to that used in the "Common Market" cases, SIECA did not merely investigate the issues from a technical point of view. It maintained continuous contact with national economic officials, and often informally exchanged ideas and negotiated with them, in an attempt to develop recommendations which would advance (or at least not undermine) integration and which would have some possibility of general acceptance. Its recommendations then served as the basis for discussions by the Economic Council. SIECA was unable, however, to persuade member countries, especially the more industrialized ones, to expand their original commitment to free trade to include measures which would effectively resolve the issue of unequal benefits and help to alleviate balance-of-payments and fiscal problems.

CENTRAL AMERICAN ECONOMIC INTEGRATION

Faced with inflexible opposition to its demands by the other member countries, the inability of SIECA to negotiate a settlement, and attempts to postpone consideration of its position, Honduras was the first to devise tactics specifically designed to force the other member countries to accede to its demands. First, it announced its refusal to deposit previously agreed-upon protocols. Still unsuccessful, it boycotted CACM meetings, thereby preventing them from being held. By so doing, it impeded the resolution of free trade problems and raised doubts concerning the degree to which it would continue to support the free trade provisions of the Common Market. It was only after it threatened to disrupt the CACM and after SIECA indicated that its demands would involve negligible economic costs that the other member countries dealt with the demands in a manner considered satisfactory by Honduras. Even then, several members refused to deposit the Protocol on Preferential Treatment for Honduras.

Honduras' use of threats to the CACM as a tactic with which to force favorable consideration of its demands encouraged the future use of similar tactics by other members. The episode demonstrated that the use of threats to the normal functioning of the Common Market did not necessarily mean disintegration and that brinkmanship tactics could be used to force the immediate and favorable consideration of a member's demands. By the late 1960's the use of threats to disrupt regional free trade had spread, and the tactics of disturbance had escalated. Members had learned to create crises in integration to gain the attention of other members for their demands for equal benefits.

Although the Central American countries have become increasingly embroiled in the controversial issue of unequal benefits derived from the Common Market--an issue common to integration efforts among developing countries--the rise in the level of controversy has not been accompanied by an increase in responsiveness to one another's needs, a growth in integrative behavior, an upgrading of the common interests of the members, or a delegation of more authority to the regional center. When some members have perceived their economic difficulties to be a consequence of or exacerbated by the structure of the Common Market and have demanded significant changes in that structure, other members, fearful of potential national economic costs, have responded by reaffirming their original commitment to free trade and to a reliance on unregulated market forces to achieve development. Regardless of the verbiage of several resolutions passed at meetings of the Economic Council and of official statements of the five Presidents, the members of the CACM have consistently been reluctant to expand or alter their commitment to include policies which would regulate market forces or involve domestic structural reforms. They have been unwilling, for example, to respond to demands from the less developed members by committing themselves to a policy of planned regional allocation of industry which would help to resolve the issue of balanced development and at the same time alleviate balance-of-payments difficulties and fiscal shortages. The combination of new demands, low level of actor responsiveness, and increasing use of tactics of brinkmanship has meant that the CACM since 1965 has bounced from crisis to crisis, each new conflict creating a greater threat to the original commitment to free trade than the conflict just preceding it. At least to date, politicization in Central America has not resulted in growth in the scope or level of integration. It has not led to significant spill-overs, only to threats of spill-backs.

On the other hand, politicization has not destroyed the CACM. The emergence of and conflicts over the issue of unequal benefits have not led to actual spill-backs--except temporarily. Why? First, the CACM has fulfilled its original commitment to free trade to such an extent that a spill-back would be costly to all members, as national economic officials have perceived. Both the level and importance of intra-regional trade to each member has grown. In the event of a breakdown, each would be forced to find new markets for its products--not an easy task. This has been perceived especially by national economic officials in the more developed member countries--El Salvador, Guatemala, and Costa Rica--which would have to locate new markets for their newly developed and Common Market-oriented manufactures. But the same holds true and to some extent is perceived by economic officials in Honduras and Nicaragua. In the absence of free trade they would be forced to find new outlets for the output from their nascent industrial plants and, more important, for their raw materials. Second, no member country seems to believe that industrialization can be achieved on the basis of its small national markets alone. Having adopted the objective of industrialization, economic officials in all five countries believe that some form of integration is necessary to bring it about, although not necessarily the present structure of integration nor integration with its present partners.

However, on the basis of the trends described earlier, there was considerable reason by mid-1969 to project a very unstable future for the CACM, a future characterized by the emergence of additional demands related to unequal benefits, low member responsiveness to such demands, the continued use of trade-disruptive devices as tactics by the dissatisfied, growing member distrust--in short, a Common Market often on the verge of collapse and promising little or no spill-over. Nothing reinforces this conclusion more clearly than the war between El Salvador and Honduras which broke out in the summer of 1969.

The CACM had never considered regional free movement of labor, the issue behind the war between Honduras and El Salvador, as within its sphere of action.[1] The General Treaty committed the five members to the free movement of goods and services but not of people. Had one of the five Ministers of Economy suggested the inclusion of a commitment to the free movement of people in the General Treaty, the other four would have either rejected it outright or simply ignored it. In a region characterized by the frequent overthrow of governments, free movement of persons is considered a political and security issue and not, like free trade, a strictly economic matter falling under the jurisdiction of the Ministries of Economy.

The free movement of persons became a more pressing as well as a more controversial issue in the 1960's. Especially over the last few decades, tens of thousands of peasants from tiny, overpopulated, large-landowner-dominated El Salvador had crossed into neighboring countries to settle on their unoccupied, generally government-owned lands. By 1965, approximately 300,000 Salvadoreans had settled in Honduras, 30,000 in Guatemala, and 12,000 in Nicaragua, most of them illegally. For El Salvador, the migration served to lessen pressures on the small, wealthy landowning elite for agrarian reform and allowed the government to focus on its policy of industrialization. A return of the migrants would have brought grave economic and uncertain political consequences. But El Salvador's neighbors also had adopted industrialization as a national objective and were not pleased with being saddled with additional peasants. Although they did not welcome the migrants, for the most part they did not take official action against them.

In March 1962, however, Honduras expelled several Salvadorean families as illegal migrants. Following a spatter of

---

[1] See Marco Tulio Zeledon, *Tercer año en la ODECA, 1962-63* (San Salvador: ODECA, 1963); Zeledon, *Cuarto año en la ODECA, 1963-64* (San Salvador: ODECA, 1964); SIECA, *Carta Informativa,* Nos. 46, 50, 64, for facts surrounding the Honduran-Salvadorean Migration Treaty of 1967. For actions taken by the Ministers of Labor and Social Security on labor mobility under ODECA auspices, see SIECA, *Carta Informativa,* No. 31. For background information about the war and for a description of the war and the immediate events which followed it, see *Latin American Newsletter* (London), 25 July, 1 August, 8 August, 5 September, 24 October, 31 October, 21 November 1969; *New York Times,* 28 June, 2 July, 4-5 July, 9 July, 15 July, 20-24 July, 26-27 July 1969; *Christian Science Monitor,* 9 July, 16-18 July, 21-25 July, 30 July 1969. The weekly editions of *Reporte Económico* (San Salvador) from June-December 1969 provide the most informed account of the war and its immediate aftermath, although from the Salvadorean point of view.

diplomatic activity, the families were allowed to return a short time later. After their return, the Secretary-General of ODECA appears to have taken the initiative and, in several meetings with the Presidents and Foreign Ministers of the two countries, to have discussed possible procedures for settling the issue of migration on a more or less permanent basis. The Secretary-General, following these preliminary meetings, formally proposed to the two Presidents that their Ministers of Interior meet to seek a solution. The ministers met and signed an agreement in June 1962 in which each pledged, among other things, not to expel nationals of the other for lack of documentation, to appoint a mixed commission to unify their migration legislation, and to reduce to a minimum the transit and residence requirements between the two countries. A few weeks later, the Presidents, Foreign Ministers, and Ministers of Interior of the two states signed the agreement. Later, the mixed commission, headed by the Ministers of Interior, negotiated a migration treaty which regularized the situation of Salvadoreans residing in Honduras and established uniform and generally easy procedures to be followed by future migrants. The two Presidents met twice to discuss the two-year treaty, signing it in late 1965. Both governments deposited the agreement in January 1967 over the objections of some Honduran unions and student groups.

While the problem of Salvadorean migrants in Honduras appeared to be at least temporarily resolved, El Salvador failed in its repeated attempts at meetings of the five Central American Presidents, in the ODECA's Council of Labor and Social Security, and before other ODECA organs to gain acceptance of the free movement of persons as a regional norm equivalent to the free movement of goods. At most, it secured agreement "in principle." National security officers rejected an ODECA plan for the free movement of persons as politically unacceptable. The Ministers of Labor suggested only that each government and ODECA gather additional information on the issue.

Soon after the agreement between Honduras and El Salvador was signed, tension between the two countries began to grow once again. The increasing numbers of semiskilled and job-competitive Salvadorean migrants to Honduras, the CACM conflict over balanced development and the long-delayed (and only Nicaraguan-induced) Salvadorean deposit of the Protocol on Preferential Treatment for Honduras, and--most important--rising demands within Honduras that the government apply the 1962 agrarian reform law beginning with government lands (on which many Salvadoreans had settled and for which, not being nationals, they were disqualified under the law) increased tensions to the point that Honduras did not extend the bilateral migration treaty when it expired in January 1969.

Occasional border incidents, a soccer competition accompanied by riots, and, finally, rumors of maltreatment by

Hondurans of Salvadorean migrants escalated the dispute over migration into a crisis resulting in the breaking of diplomatic relations in June. At this point, Honduran authorities, no longer bound by the 1967 treaty and in the initial stages of implementing the 1962 agrarian reform law, began to expel some "illegal" Salvadorean migrants. As a result of harassment or expulsion, approximately 14,000 Salvadoreans fled Honduras during the following three weeks.

Only at this stage, after the breaking of diplomatic relations, an increase in the number of border incidents, and complaints by El Salvador to the OAS, did the Foreign Ministers of Guatemala, Nicaragua, and Costa Rica intervene to try to mediate the dispute.[2] The three suggested a peace plan which included a migration treaty at the Central American level according to which excess population would be allowed to migrate to areas of less density with favorable conditions for agricultural and industrial settlement. Until that time the three had opposed such an agreement on migration. In any case, their plan was offered too late. After Honduras had expelled thousands of Salvadoreans, the Salvadorean government escalated its demands from a Honduran guarantee of permanence for the migrants to a demand that Honduras pay indemnifications. After a growing exodus of migrants and an increasing number of grave border incidents, El Salvador attacked Honduras on July 14.

The war continued until a seven-man commission appointed by the OAS, headed by the Nicaraguan Foreign Minister, and including the Costa Rican and Guatemalan Foreign Ministers, worked out a cease-fire agreement on July 18. By that time, several

---

[2]The same day on which El Salvador broke diplomatic relations with Honduras, it lodged a complaint with the OAS asking it to intervene to prevent the violation of the human rights of Salvadoreans residing in Honduras. The Secretary-General of the OAS asked two of the members of the Inter-American Human Rights Commission to visit both of the countries during 30 June-6 July. It was at this point that the three Central American Foreign Ministers offered to act as interim mediators. They remained trying to mediate the dispute while the members of the Human Rights Commission investigated the affair. The Commission arrived late (approximately July 12) and issued no report, opening itself to Salvadorean attacks. Meanwhile, Honduras charged El Salvador with aggression early in July, and El Salvador made countercharges. At an emergency session of the Permanent Council of the OAS on July 4, the delegates agreed to allow the three Central American Foreign Ministers additional time to mediate the affair through ODECA. The Foreign Ministers were engaged in that task when war broke out on July 14.

CONCLUSION

thousands on both sides had been killed, about one-half of El Salvador's oil refining and storage capacity had been destroyed, and a significant portion of Honduran territory had been occupied by Salvadorean troops. The OAS commission was able to stop the fighting, but faced with demands by El Salvador for iron-clad guarantees for the protection of Salvadoreans residing in Honduras and for indemnifications, it was unable to bring about a Salvadorean withdrawal. However, after an OAS Emergency Meeting of Foreign Ministers decided to apply rigorous economic sanctions against El Salvador unless it left Honduran territory, El Salvador withdrew its troops late in July.

Several attempts by an OAS mediator to negotiate a permanent peace settlement between the two countries broke down after sporadic fighting again took place in February 1970. A later effort by an OAS committee also reached an impasse. Finally, in June 1970 Honduras and El Salvador agreed to a plan worked out by the five Central American Foreign Ministers, acting under the auspices of the OAS, which established a demilitarized zone on each side of their border, policed by small security patrols provided by the other Central American countries and financed by the OAS.

In what way does a knowledge of the events surrounding the war enlighten us about the process of Central American integration? Most important, it indicates the extent to which there is a lack of perceived interdependence between economic and security policy areas by decision-makers in the Central American countries, and the dangers of such a condition for the maintenance of an integration effort.

In the years preceding the war, most national decision-makers perceived the migration issue as primarily a security matter. Economic officials, therefore, did not participate in regional discussions of the problem, although the economic consequences of any resolution or even nonresolution of the problem would be considerable. At the same time, economic officials generally controlled integration affairs. National security officers and Foreign Ministers remained largely uninvolved in the process. What is startling is the extent to which national policy-making was unintegrated, and the extent to which national decision-makers in one issue-area operated autonomously from decision-makers in other seemingly closely related issue-areas.

One consequence of this pattern of national decision-making was that even after nine years of close contact between Salvadorean and Honduran economic officials and after a considerable growth in the interdependence of their two economies (with El Salvador dependent on Honduras as a main outlet for the products from its new plants), political and military leaders who made the decision to go to war in 1969 over the migration issue acted as though they were unaware of this growing economic interdependence. It appears that they did not consult with economic officials on the economic consequences of belligerency. Thus, although the separation of some economic issues from security affairs in Central America gave economic officials some leeway in managing national entry into the CACM in the early 1960's, in 1969 it meant that economic officials had no control over the events which led to war and those who had control were unfamiliar with the facts of or in any case unaffected by the experience of economic integration.[3]

What have been the short-term consequences and what will be the long-range significance of the war for the future of integration in Central America? One immediate consequence has been the inability of the Economic and Executive Councils to meet for more than a year. This has meant that unresolved conflicts which arose before the war have grown more complex. Nicaragua, for example, has continued to apply its consumption tax in a manner the others hold to be discriminatory. New "Common Market problems" have arisen since the war. Costa Rica, alleging discrimination especially by Nicaragua, has imposed the equivalent of tariffs on imports of clothing and oats from the rest of Central America. In retaliation, each of the other members has imposed import duty bonds on all Costa Rican products. SIECA has had only limited success in attempting to resolve these and similar problems on a bilateral basis. As a result of these conflicts, the rate of growth of intra-regional trade has diminished. In addition, for months after the end of the war, Honduras refused to allow passage of Salvadorean goods through its territory. El Salvador, at least in the short-run, lost not only its lucrative Honduran market but a part of its markets in Nicaragua and Costa Rica as well. In sum, in the year since the war, trading patterns within the region have significantly shifted.

Even should passage of Salvadorean goods through Honduras be made more secure and should the CACM organs meet (both likely occurrences in the near future), the long-term problems which the postwar Common Market faces are indeed grave. First, even should regional free trade be reestablished, trade between El Salvador and Honduras at least for some time to come can be expected to be at a much lower level than prior to the war. Nationals in each country will not be as willing to consume one another's products

---

[3]See the well-supported argument by Nye that this "separability" of economic matters from the mainstream of political debate" in the Central American countries was an important factor in the successful initiation of the CACM. Nye, "Central American Economic Integration," pp. 393-394.

as they were before. Charges of discrimination can be expected
to follow and to cause conflicts. Second, and more serious, the
increase in nationalist sentiments in El Salvador, the most developed, and in Honduras, the least developed country in the region, can be expected to increase the salience of the still-un-
resolved conflicts over unequal benefits and to increase the
likelihood that additional, similar demands will arise in the
future. Although the issue of unequal benefits will emerge more
frequently and will be even more controversial than during the
recent past, the rise in the nationalist sentiments of two of
the members and the general distrust of the market's stability
will mean that all members will be even less responsive to one
another's needs and demands and even less successful than in the
past in resolving such conflicts. After superimposing these new
developments onto the past trends, the best that can be expected
in the postwar Common Market will be some restoration of free
trade with a more tentative national commitment to regional free
trade than previously, the emergence and nonresolution of additional conflicts over unequal benefits, a lower degree of mutual
responsiveness, and an increased probability of a spill-back to
bilateral or trilateral free trade agreements. The outlook for
the future is indeed bleak.

BIBLIOGRAPHY

Abelardo Delgado, Pedro (Secretary-General, SIECA). Letter to
    Minister of Economy, Honduras, August 2, 1965. Mimeo.

ANDI (National Association of Industrialists, Honduras). Nota
    No. 949, 3 de diciembre de 1964. Mimeo.

Banco Central de Costa Rica. Memoria anual: 1967--La economía
    nacional. San José, 1968.

Barrera, Mario, and Haas, Ernst B. "The Operationalization of
    Some Variables Related to Regional Integration," Interna-
    tional Organization, Vol. XXIII, No. 1 (Winter 1969).

Cable, Vincent. "Problems in the Central American Common Market,"
    Review, Bank of London and South America, Vol. 3, No. 30
    (June 1969).

Castillo, Carlos. Growth and Integration in Central America.
    New York: Praeger, 1966.

CCE (Committee on Economic Cooperation). "Exposición sobre la
    participación de Honduras en el proceso de integración
    económica centroamericana." CCE/IX/D.T.2.

Christian Science Monitor. 5 December 1968; 9 July, 16-18 July,
    21-25 July, and 30 July 1969.

Comercio Exterior, Vol. 19, No. 3 (March 1969).

Consejo Monetario Centroamericano. Boletín Estadístico, Año I,
    No. 1 (1965), Año III, No. 3 (1966), Año IV, No. 4 (1967),
    Año V, No. 5 (1968).

Dell, Sidney. "The Early Years of LAFTA" in M. Wionczek, ed.,
    Latin American Economic Integration: Experiences and Pros-
    pects. New York: Praeger, 1966.

ECLA (Economic Commission for Latin America). Economic Survey
    of Latin America, 1965. E/CN.12/752/Rev. 1.

_____. The Latin American Economy in 1967. E/CN.12/806.

The Economist para América Latina, Vol. 2, No. 22 (October 1968),
    and Vol. 2, No. 23 (November 1968).

BIBLIOGRAPHY

El Día (Tegucigalpa), 25 October 1965.

First National City Bank of New York, Foreign Information Service.
    "A Progress Report: The Central American Common Market."
    New York: June 1967.

General Treaty for Central American Economic Integration. Guate-
    mala City: SIECA, 1964.

Gonzalez del Valle, Jorge. "Monetary Integration in Central
    America: Achievements and Expectations," Journal of Common
    Market Studies, Vol. V, No. 1 (September 1966).

Haas, Ernst B. "The Study of Regional Integration: Somber Re-
    flections on the Joy and Anguish of Pre-Theorizing," Inter-
    national Organization, Vol. XXIV, No. 4 (Autumn 1970).

_____, and Schmitter, Philippe C. "Economics and Differential
    Patterns of Political Integration: Projections about Unity
    in Latin America," International Organization, Vol. XVIII, No.
    4 (August 1964). Also in H. Bull et al., International Polit-
    ical Communities: An Anthology. New York: Doubleday, 1966.

Hansen, Roger D. Central America: Regional Integration and Eco-
    nomic Development. Washington: National Planning Associa-
    tion, Studies in Development Progress, No. 1, 1967.

_____. "Regional Integration: Reflections on a Decade of
    Theoretical Efforts," World Politics, Vol. XXI, No. 2
    (January 1969).

IIEJI (Instituto Interamericano de Estudios Jurídicos Interna-
    cionales). Derecho comunitario centroamericano. San José,
    Costa Rica, 1968.

INTAL (Instituto para la Integración de América Latina). La
    integración económica de América Latina. Buenos Aires,
    1968. English translation: The Economic Integration of
    Latin America. Buenos Aires: Talleres Graficos, 1968.

International Organization, Vol. XXIV, No. 4 (Autumn 1970).
    Articles by Hayward Alker, Donald Puchala, Joseph S. Nye,
    and Ernst B. Haas.

Jalloh, Abdul A. "Neo-Functionalism and Regional Political Inte-
    gration in Africa," Yale University, 1970. Unpublished.

La Gaceta, Diario Oficial de Nicaragua, 21 June 1968.

La Industria (Tegucigalpa), July 1965. Report on the First Joint
    Meeting.

BIBLIOGRAPHY

Latin American Newsletter (London). 12 July and 27 December 1968; 21 February, 28 February, 14 March, 28 March, 25 April, 27 June, 25 July, 1 August, 8 August, 5 September, 24 October, 31 October, and 21 November 1969.

Levine, Meldon E. "The Private Sector and the Common Market," Woodrow Wilson School of Public and International Affairs, Princeton University, October 1965. Unpublished.

Martínez, Práxedes. Article in La Industria, National Industrial Association of Honduras, November 1964.

New York Times. 20 January, 28 June, 2 July, 4-5 July, 9 July, 15 July, 20-24 July, and 26-27 July 1969.

Nye, Joseph S. "Central American Economic Integration" in Joseph S. Nye, ed., International Regionalism. Boston: Little, Brown, 1968.

_____. "Comparative Regional Integration: Concept and Measurement," International Organization, Vol. XXII, No. 4 (Autumn 1968).

_____. "Patterns and Catalysts in Regional Integration" in Joseph S. Nye, ed., International Regionalism. Boston: Little, Brown, 1968.

Reporte Económico (El Salvador). 24 May, 7 June, 14 June, 21 June, 28 June, 2 August, 15 November, 22 November, and 13 December 1968; 7 March, 14 March, 28 March, 25 April, and 6 June 1969; June-December 1969.

Schmitter, Philippe C. "La dinámica de contradicciones y la conducción de crisis en la integración centroamericana," Revista de la Integración, No. 5 (November 1969).

_____. "Further Notes on Operationalizing Some Variables Related to Regional Integration," International Organization, Vol. XXIII, No. 2 (Spring 1969).

_____. "The Process of Central American Integration: Spill-Over or Spill-Around?" Berkeley: University of California, Institute of International Studies. Mimeo.

_____. "A Revised Theory of International Integration," International Organization, Vol. XXIV, No. 4 (Autumn 1970).

_____. "Three Neo-Functional Hypotheses about International Integration," International Organization, Vol. XXIII, No. 1 (Winter 1969).

BIBLIOGRAPHY

Secretaria de Economía y Hacienda, República de Honduras. Notas Nos. 255 and 356, 10 de diciembre de 1964. Mimeo.

Segal, Aaron. "The Integration of Developing Countries: Some Thoughts on East Africa and Central America," Journal of Common Market Studies, Vol. V, No. 3 (March 1967).

Sidjanski, Dusan. Dimensiones institucionales de la integración latinoamericana. Buenos Aires: INTAL, 1967.

SIECA (Permanent Secretariat of Central American Economic Integration). Carta Informativa, 1964-69. Nos. 28, 31, 33, 39, 40-42, 46, 49-50, 52, 57, 60, 63-64, 66 (Anexo Estadístico No. 61), 74, 78-79, 80-85, 87-90, 92, 92 (Anexo Estadístico No. 87), 93.

_____. "Comentarios de la SIECA al pronunciamiento de la Asociación Nacional de Industriales de Honduras." Enclosed with letter from Pedro Abelardo Delgado to Minister of Economy, Honduras, August 2, 1965. Mimeo.

_____. Comentarios sobre les rubros pendientes de equiparación arancelaria. Nota de la Secretaria, SIECA/CE-XV/64. Guatemala, June 1965.

USAID (U.S. Agency for International Development), Regional Office for Central America and Panama. Economic Integration Treaties of Central America. Guatemala City, 1966.

U.S. Department of State, American Embassy, El Salvador. "Summary of Economic Conditions," First Quarter 1965. Mimeo.

_____. American Embassy, Guatemala. "Economic Survey," First Quarter 1965. Mimeo.

_____. American Embassy, Honduras. "Economic Survey," Fourth Quarter 1964.

Wardlaw, Andrew B. "The Operations of the Central American Common Market." Guatemala City: Regional Office for Central Americ and Panama, USAID, 1966. Mimeo.

Wionczek, Miguel. "Introduction: Requisites for Viable Integration" in M. Wionczek, ed., Latin American Economic Integration: Experiences and Prospects. New York: Praeger, 1966.

Young, John Parke. Central American Monetary Union. Guatemala City: Regional Office for Central America and Panama, USAID, 1965.